Foreword

GW01451291

Belonging

The inner journey of being fully
seen, known & loved

Rory Helart

Thank you

I want to first thank my wife Mari for her endless support as I wrote this book and her voice of strength and wisdom in every season of my life. I am forever grateful for a wife who has stood by my side as I have had to process and overcome the different seasons, painful experiences, and people that have affected my life. I would not be the man I am today without you. I want to thank one of my best friends Donta for his constant belief in me and this project and for always being a safe place and one of my people who knows everything about me. To my three children Brooklyn, Harper, and Kinsley, I pray my ceiling will become your floor and the breakthroughs in my life will set you up to run faster, soar higher, and see God move in your life in greater ways than I have. To Tom and Leslie, thank you for your mentorship in my life and constant voice to trust in God even in seasons when I wanted to give up and quit. To Carling, my editor and friend who has helped make this book come to life. And finally to our Young Saints staff and leaders, thank you for your constant belief in me and trust in my leadership. You are truly the dream team and my joy to run with.

Endorsements

"Throughout history, God has raised up leaders who carry a message of love and power that awakens a generation. The message is always an invitation to encounter the radical love of Jesus and experience the freedom that is found only in Him. The result is a generation firmly secure in their identity in Christ and unshakeable in the midst of any storm. Rory is one of those leaders in this generation. It has been such a joy to see how God has used his life so powerfully to lead a generation into encounters with the radical and extravagant love of the Father. The truth that Rory shares is not just a theory he read in a book but a first-hand experience he has encountered for himself. God is using His life to set people free and invite them to a place of truly belonging."

–Banning Liebscher
Jesus Culture Founder and Lead Pastor
Author of: *Jesus Culture; The Three-Mile Walk; Rooted*

"*Belonging* is a beautifully written and deeply insightful guide to discovering how to overcome pain and step back into intimacy with both God and those around us. Rory masterfully weaves personal stories with profound wisdom, offering readers a roadmap to understanding and embracing how to walk in forgiveness and become a resting place of the Holy Spirit. This book is a must-read for anyone seeking to cultivate genuine connections and a sense of belonging in their lives. It not only inspires but also provides practical tools for building meaningful relationships. I wholeheartedly recommend *Belonging* to anyone on the path to finding their true community and home."

–Dawna De Silva
Bethel Sozo Founder and Co-Leader
Author of: *Sozo: Saved, Healed, Delivered; Shifting Atmospheres; Overcoming Fear; Warring with Wisdom*

"Rory Helart is a powerful influencer to teens, youth leaders, and parents of teens, but he has a needed message for all generations. I highly recommend his book, *Belonging*. In it, he gives powerful insights for victory by sharing how he overcame rejection, negative self-talk, and the lies that limited his peace and connection with others. *Belonging* is a timely book to help us all embrace the joy and fulfillment of deep connection with others. Thanks, Rory, for your life and message. It is making a difference."

–Steve Backlund
Co-Founder of Igniting Hope Ministries

"Whole and Healthy people are going to change the world, the ones armed with the truth of who God is, and how He sees me. Rory has created a road map to living a life of belonging and wholeness. I want to encourage you to read this with an open heart as this could be the breakthrough that you have been looking for. We need people and people need the best version of us. This is the book to help you get there."

–Ben Serpell
Senior Leader at Loving On Purpose

"One of the great mysteries of the gospel is that Christ Jesus dwells and reveals His glory in ordinary men and women who surrender their lives to Him. The human experience is not just important to God, but is His chosen conduit for His power to flow through and to reveal His nature and likeness in. We often forget how deeply God cares for us, our story, and our struggles and fail to realize that in Himself–God has made every provision for us to be healed, restored, and walk in the freedom of His great love for us. Rory has written and articulated the incredible and vulnerable invitation we all have to bring our true hearts to Jesus and find His voice and nearness in the places we would prefer to hide. *Belonging* is a book for us all, and will equip us as the body to walk under the leadership of Jesus and in the freedom and life He paid for."

–Hayley Braun
Senior Leader at Bethel Church; BSSM 3rd year Overseer
Author of: *Surrendered to the Holy Spirit*

"Rory Helart is experienced in reaching the next generation. He served faithfully, and wholeheartedly on my team for 15 years till I passed the baton of Young Saints off to him. I have watched him flourish, grow as a son, and overcome the personal challenges he writes about in the book. Discovering *Belonging* will help you overcome rejection and encounter the Lord, and grow in your relationship with God."

–Tom Crandall
Senior Leader of Bethel Church; Evangelism Director
Author of: *Your Life Speaks*

Contents

Foreword

In every heart, there is a deep and unshakable longing to belong—to be known, loved, and accepted without reservation. This desire is more than a fleeting emotion; it is a profound spiritual reality that echoes the very nature of God. In *Belonging*, Rory Helart takes us on a powerful journey into the heart of this longing, inviting us to explore what it means to truly belong in the presence of our Creator.

Rory's story is more than a collection of personal experiences; it is an invitation to every reader to step into the transformative power of God's love. As I read the pages of this book, I was struck by the depth of vulnerability and honesty that Rory shares. He doesn't shy away from the struggles of rejection, insecurity, and the pain of not feeling enough—struggles that many of us, including myself, face in our own lives. Yet, it is through these very struggles that God often does His most profound work, leading us from a place of isolation to one of deep connection and belonging.

This book is more than just a guide; it is a companion on the journey of faith. Rory weaves together personal stories, biblical insights, and practical steps to help you navigate the road to belonging. His experiences are a testament to the healing and freedom that come when we allow God to touch the most hidden parts of our hearts!

In a world where many are searching for their place, Belonging is a timely and necessary message. It speaks to the core of who we are as children of God, reminding us that our identity is not found in what we do, but in who we are in Him. Rory's journey is a reminder that no matter where we have been or what we have faced, there is a victorious place for us in the Father's heart.

As you read this book, my prayer is that you will be encouraged to take your own steps toward finding the belonging you were created for. May Rory's words inspire you to face the pain, confront the lies, and embrace the truth of who you are in Christ. Let this be the season where you find your place, not just in the world, but in the glorious presence of the One who loves you beyond measure.

Welcome to Belonging. May your journey be as transformative as Rory's has been!

–Kris Vallotton

Prologue

Life is a road full of ups and downs that if we learn how to navigate, can take us deeper into the place we are called to live, the place of His glorious Presence. I began writing this book after an encounter I had with the Lord that led me to a series of encounters that have changed my life and walk with God forever. I want to take a moment to share some of the significant encounters that led me to find and discover the things I have written about in this book and hopefully will set you up with a vision for what you are about to access by reading this book. The first of these encounters was in 2020 during a time of chaos in the nation I am from and worldwide shutdowns. I had a vision that there was a book with a title on it called Belonging. I then heard a voice say, "I need you to write this book." I wish I could tell you I got right to it, but as I have discovered in the last fours years, God first had to deal with all the places in me where I didn't feel I belonged.

For most of my adult life I have fought the lies of not feeling good enough, being rejected by people, struggling with consistent insecurities, and not knowing how to confidently show up as me. I struggled to access what God had paid for, but was aware that the way I was living didn't feel like the promise of His Presence that seemed available. I pondered the book title and received many prophetic words after that to write the book, but I wasn't prepared for what would happen in my life next.

In October of 2022, I was in a youth service and the Holy Spirit was thick in the room. One of our core team leaders was speaking in our junior high service on being yielded to the Holy Spirit. As He was speaking, tears started to fill my eyes and the presence of God was thick around me. I was trying to figure out what was going on, as I knew I wasn't feeling sad. The service finished and I had to step out to handle a situation. Our high school service began, and as my good friend Donta started speaking, tears streamed down my face almost uncontrollably during his message. I started to feel like I was distracting the room by how heavy my crying was as I lay on the floor weeping. Donta was also speaking on yielding to the Holy Spirit. As

I began to cry even louder I heard the Father say to me, "I am requiring something from you tonight." I answered and said, "I will give you anything." Then I heard Him say, "Your shield of 'Protector.'" Instantly I felt my body pull back and resist the Holy Spirit. In my mind, I started to rationalize why this would be a bad idea. Instantly, images of different people came to mind that I knew I would no longer be able to protect. I then realized being a protector was wrapped up in my identity. It was a part of who I was as a person. I then heard the Father say, "I will be your Protector." I started weeping heavily as I surrendered the shield. I saw for a moment that I was holding on to a shield and I let go of it and watched it fall off me. I instantly felt exposed and vulnerable. That feeling didn't go away for a season, as the Lord was getting ready to change my life forever.

A few weeks later, in November of 2022, I was in a youth service again. A friend of mine was speaking that night, and to be honest, the room of teens felt tired and they were struggling to engage. It was a weird moment for me as I felt God strongly to invite this friend to speak, and my friend felt God stirring him to release something that night, yet the room was flat. The service ended and my friend grabbed his team and they prayed. Youth were starting to exit the sanctuary and my friend said, "Maybe we should just pray for the leaders while we are here." I agreed and found myself kneeling on the ground, face down. I wish I could say I was feeling the Presence of God, but in reality, I was thinking about eating a burger when we were done praying. My mind was rapidly going from thought to thought and I felt no anticipation of this moment. That's when it happened.

My friend called for me to crawl over to my wife who was being prayed for. I went to move and realized I felt as though I weighed 500 pounds. My mind started racing as I realized I was unable to move even a finger. Nothing was working. As I opened my mouth to try and speak I started screaming in tongues. A sense of fear filled my thoughts as I realized God was all around me and I was unaware. The moment I stopped trying to speak, a voice spoke loud and sure over me. "Rory I want to put my glory on you, but I have to deal with the pain inside of you, or my glory will crush you." That night I was in a three and a half hour encounter where I couldn't move or speak, but I was covered in the glory of God as He revealed and healed areas of pain and bad beliefs that had riddled my life. I came out of that encounter as a different person. These first two encounters launched me into a season of encounters, surrender, facing pain, forgiveness, and finding my true identity outside of a call, position, or gift. On the other side, I have found a place in God I have been searching for my whole life.

This was the season I laid down false protections and false identities, faced my unresolved pain, forgave, got honest, and allowed God and people to see every part of me. The good, bad, and ugly. It was the season I discovered the confidence that comes from knowing you are fully seen, known, and loved by God and by the people closest to you in your life. This was the season I began to fully understand belonging.

My prayer for you as you read this book is that you would go on your own journey of facing hard truths and unresolved seasons and spaces of pain and unforgiveness in order to find healing in His presence and the weight of His glory on your life. His glory is weighty, which leaves no room for any additional weight. I pray that you would leave no stone unturned and no season untouched–allowing the Holy Spirit to set your life up as His temple for His glory to rest in. I pray this is the season for you to experience the glory of God–His physical manifest Presence in your life.

Chapter 1:
What is Belonging?

What was I doing? My heart was racing, nerves para-
lyzed my body, and I was struggling to form conscious
thoughts. I had never done anything like this before. There
I found myself on my way to my first church camp experience. This was not my ideal place to be, I struggled with
social anxiety, insecurity, bullying, and pain from rejection
and loneliness in my life. I was only on that bus because a
girl I liked had invited me and it made me feel wanted. The
camp commenced and I was proactively placing myself
in spaces where I could hide. I didn't believe in this God
stuff anyway, and I had already experienced so much
pain and hypocrisy growing up from church and leaders, I

was convinced it was all a show. I was just there because of this girl.

It was the third night of the youth camp, and the first two nights were heavy repentance alter calls. My walls were up every time the call was given as I was convinced this was an emotional show to manipulate people, and I was not going to be controlled. This third night was different, the lead pastor called it, being quiet in the Presence of God. I had never heard of such a thing, but I was grateful that we were all told to sit and listen. Then the lead pastor said, "If there is anything else that anyone needs prayer for we would love to take this time to pray for you." I went to check out and then something happened. A loud voice ricocheted through the room, "RORY!" I looked around in panic and embarrassment. My goal was to hide, and now someone had just yelled my name in a quiet moment. As I began looking around no one else seemed to have heard it, I pondered what was happening and then two thoughts hit my mind that changed my life forever. *God is real and He knows my name.* That was the night I came into a radical revelation of God and surrendered my life to Him. It was the first time I received a glimpse of what belonging in His glory could look like.

What is Belonging?

When I think of the word belonging, I imagine a state of being where a person discovers who they truly are created to be, and from that place allows themselves to be fully seen, loved, and known. Now imagine that level of visibility within the glory of God, His manifest Presence. The people who discover how to find and live out of that place walk with authentic confidence, secure identity, and a life that flows with healing and freedom. **The person who has truly discovered the secret of belonging is undoubtedly the most confident person in the room.** Belonging isn't just a good thought, but a need placed deep within humanity that, if not fulfilled, leads us down many roads we were never meant to walk on.

Many people today are searching for belonging. People join groups, start movements, create wealth, or join teams in an attempt to find a place where they feel they belong. In a time when family has brought more pain sometimes than benefits, and churches have hurt almost as many people as they have helped, it's time to ask ourselves, what is the thing we are all searching for that we are having a hard time finding? We have to discover that external circumstances never change internal realities. While being a part of a team, in a group, with a family, or in a church, are all good things, if our internal world doesn't feel like we truly belong, our external circumstances will only become a band-aid for the pain, not a healer for it. If we never address the pain and disconnection inside of us, we create it around us in our lives.

We must face our internal world to truly discover what is holding us back from the life we are designed to live. The encounter I had at that youth camp started my journey to face the scary pain, sin, disappointment, betrayal in relationships, unforgiveness, and darkness inside of me that I had never told anyone about. This journey didn't happen that night, it only began that night. I started down the path to discover who created me and why. It is a path that is well-worn by other men and women who have gone before us to show what is possible for the person who truly finds belonging in God's glory. The place where nothing is hidden, there is no shame, and the person finds perfect peace and confidence in the manifest Presence of God.

Never Lost

The start of this journey comes with an eye-opening revelation. Many people think that when you get saved is the beginning of God watching you, being with you, and being aware of you. This couldn't be farther from the truth. God is constantly pursuing us before we ever surrender our lives to Him. There is a phrase in the church that we "go after the lost." I believe it has created a weird belief that God has lost someone when that just isn't true. God sees everything and we only find Him because He is already pursuing us. He is just waiting for the moment when we let Him in, and our guards come down. When that happens we discover what has already been happening all along. God is an ever-present reality all around us. He loves us more than we love Him. On this journey of finding belonging and walking in confidence, we need to discover that He has been and always will be thinking of us. We are special and full of purpose from the moment of conception. We are the apple of His eye, and He delights in us.

This idea of God's radical love can be hard to comprehend in a world full of pain, chaos, and disillusionment. We have to remember that fathers establish value and God being our Father set up a value system even from our conception. In the beginning, we were made in His image, and at conception, He actively formed us.

> For you formed my inmost parts; you wove me in my mother's womb. I will give thanks to You, for I am

fearfully and wonderfully made; wonderful are Your works, and my soul knows it very well. My frame was not hidden from you, when I was made in secret, and skillfully wrought in the depths of the earth; your eyes have seen my unformed substance; and in Your book were all written the days that were ordained for me, when as yet there was not one of them. How precious also are Your thoughts to me, O God! How vast is the sum of them! If I should count them, they would outnumber the sand. When I awake, I am still with You (Psalm 139:13-18).

He is already invested in every human, desiring for them to find Him–the place they belong. For many, the revelation of God as a loving, good Father has been a journey to understand–a journey that I hope is enhanced by the pages of this book. God is real and He knows your name. We can only love Him because He already loves us. We can only choose Him because He already has chosen us. John 3:16 isn't just a church verse for kids. It is the revelation of the lengths God has gone to create a way for us to be with Him. It is a way for us to get back to the Garden of Eden, where humanity first walked with God fully seen, known, loved, and in the place of belonging.

As you read the beginning of this book, you may be thinking, "I feel like I already belong. I'm not sure I need what you are talking about." While that may be true, let me pose a few questions to reveal if you have found the true sense of belonging that is available for every person created. Have you ever thought, "If people knew this about me they would probably never see me the same?" Or, "If I shared this part of my past I wouldn't have the opportunities I have now." Or maybe, "If people actually knew me, they wouldn't like me." Let's go even deeper, "When the Presence of God fills a room am I at rest or anxious? Do I feel confident or do I need to do something spiritual to feel good enough to be there?" "Have God and I talked about my past? Or do I act like He doesn't know it?" These are just a few questions we can ask ourselves to discover if we are struggling with our place of belonging.

Over the years countless people have come into my office struggling with feelings of disconnection, social anxiety, locked-up pain from past seasons, fear of vulnerability, cycles, struggles, and disconnection from God. You name it, it has come up. I have had people grip a coffee table in my office in anguish as they are trying to get out through a whisper, painful scary things they have done or things that have been done to them that have plagued them for years and sometimes decades, keeping them from a place of belonging. They have tried to forget these things and have even imagined that God doesn't want to see them. But once it's all brought into the light, the breath of freedom and relief floods my office as they discover that the thing that felt like a dragon was only a mirage. It is time to find the path of unbroken fellowship with the Father who created us and loves us–the place where we no longer have to prove anything to God or to ourselves. "If anyone loves Me, he will keep My word; and My Father will love him, and We will come to him and make our abode with Him" (John 14:23). The Godhead is ready to make His home in us and our lives a resting place for His glory.

Counting the Higher Cost

Many people desire the idea of belonging but don't realize that the cost of not pursuing it leads them to walk out an unfulfilled, insecure, striving life where pain and people dictate who they are and what they become. It has cost people their peace, joy, friendships, connections, victories, destinies, relationships, families, confidence, fulfillment, and even their own identities. The cost is great and I have paid my share of its price too many times. I and so many others I have walked with have discovered that the benefits and freedom that exist on the other side of facing these hard things far outweigh the momentary fear and uneasiness that comes from facing the pain. Nothing worth receiving ever comes easy. God never promised an easy life, but He did make a life of perfect connection with Him and freedom available to us. This is the life of belonging.

My heart for you reading this book is that you would gain keys and insight to help you access the life that Jesus paid for and that you would find the path to a life of belonging in God's presence–the life of unbroken fellowship– being fully seen, fully known, and fully loved. The life of radical confidence, because you are connected to a wonderful Father. I pray that through this book you would have a revelation of the Father's love that would bypass beliefs, barriers, and comforts that have been used to try and get you outside of the place you have always belonged. The place of oneness and perfect communion with God our Father.

Meditation Questions

1. How do I know God is real?
2. Am I confident that God knows me? Does that feel like a good thing?
3. Is there something in my past that I try to imagine didn't happen?
4. Is there something that I have done or something that was done to me that I have never told anyone?
5. Do I feel that if people actually knew me, they wouldn't like me? Explain
6. When the Presence of God fills a room am I at rest or anxious? Do I feel confident or do I need to do something spiritual to feel good enough to be there?
7. Have God and I talked about my past or do I act like he doesn't know it or parts of it?

The Path Forward

1. Find one friend and one mentor to go on this journey of belonging with. The first step is taking the risk to let someone into what you are going after.
2. Spend time alone in silence each week with God. Use a journal to record your journey of stepping out of isolation, pain, anxiety, and fear, and into the connection, confidence, freedom, and belonging God has for you.

Chapter 2:
Discovering the
Nature of God

Is God defined by my experiences? Most people have never stopped long enough even to ponder the answer to this question. The majority of people live their lives in reaction mode and many in survival mode. Why do we do this? God is good, right? He is loving, right? But many times our experiences in life don't always play out the way we want them to. One of the greatest challenges people of faith face regardless of social status, finance, opportunity, favor, or any other thing that makes life easier, is discovering how to hold onto and find the true nature of God in the midst of circumstances, situations, or painful life events that don't line up with the nature we have heard. **On the path to belonging, we have to discover the God we want to belong to.** How do we start this? How do we reconcile all the bad things in the world and all the pain, loss, sadness, disappointment, and grief? How do we reconcile when leaders, friends, ministries, and churches hurt us?

Who is in Control?

There was a young woman named Paisley who found herself in my office one day. I had known her at this point for a few years and one thing was certain, fear of bad things happening to her and the people she loved was preventing her from fully living the life she dreamed of. As we sat down I knew this could be a pretty intense meeting. As we started the journey to discover what was causing the strong irrational fears to flair up and the vivid pictures in her mind to flash of horrific things happening to her or people she loved, we hit a point that revealed the next big breakthrough of Paisley's life. I asked her to imagine the throne of God and to see God the Father sitting on His throne. As she sat on the couch in my office that day she had a self-revelation on her journey of belonging. Tears streamed down her face as she said, "I see myself on the throne. What does that mean?" I knew exactly what that meant–she was living like she was in control of her life. We as humans were never designed to live in this state as being the ones in full control of our lives. Why? Because if we really stop to think of it, we don't have control over many areas of our lives. We can't control life, death, family, or friends. The Bible even says it is hard for a man to control his tongue (James 1:26). When a person doesn't understand the true nature of God and in fear grasps for control of their life we start to see the effects of that decision show up almost instantly through fear, panic, self-protection, guardedness, they are emotionally distant from people, slow to trust in relationships, they struggle to make friends, have trouble sleeping, and the list goes on. How do I know these things? Apart from the countless people I have sat with in my office over the last decade to help them walk through this, I have also had to face my own internal struggles with panic, anxiety, control, fear, relationship struggles, you name it, I've lived it. **The next key on this journey to finding belonging is to surrender the mystery of reality to embrace the Truth of the eternal.**

Embracing Mystery

The mystery of reality is the space of no resolve that

creates mystery in our lives and sometimes tension in our walk with God–it is the circumstances that create questions like, why do godly people get sick? Why do children die? Why are my finances not where I thought they would be? Why am I not married? Do I have a purpose? Why did that church leader hurt me so bad? Why didn't God come through? Why did God let this happen?

Why? Why? Why? The questions are endless.

When our brains can't reconcile something we go into what is called a loop. This is where the brain continues to dwell and meditate on a certain scenario trying to find a resolve only to discover that it cannot find one. This is where people get stuck in life. It can be a traumatic event or a long road of disappointment. **Whatever the cause, there are moments where life and the nature of God don't line up, and we have to decide what reality to believe.** Do we believe in the nature of God when it's experienced or because it's true? We are designed to walk with God and belong to Him. We are created to be connected and abiding with our Father. But when we have a question looping in our brain that is warring against the nature of God, we find that the last place we want to run to is His Presence. This is the battle that 2 Corinthians 10:3-5 talks about: "For though we walk in the flesh, we do not war according to the flesh, for the weapons of our warfare are not of the flesh, but divinely powerful for the destruction of fortresses. We are destroying speculations and every lofty thing raised up against the knowledge of God, and we are taking every thought captive to the obedience of Christ."

The words that we need to become acquainted with are "speculations" and "lofty things", raised up against the knowledge of God. The word "speculations" is the Greek word "logismos" and can mean reckoning, reasoning, or judgment.[1] The word "lofty" is the Greek word "hypsoma" and means 'a thing elevated.'[2] Paul is warning believers that thoughts will enter our minds that tempt us to reason, judge, and elevate thoughts above the knowledge and nature of God. How could a thought become that powerful? How does someone find themselves warring with thoughts that would reason against God's nature or worse, judge His nature?

I'll tell you a personal story to help illustrate this point and how someone can find themselves warring in their thoughts when circumstances and life don't seem to match up with the God we believe in.

The Moment of True Surrender

It was October 2010 and I had just taken a big leap of faith to follow the Lord to move to a new city. I was 21, had been dating my now wife for a year at this point, and was on the verge of proposing when this sudden move was placed in my path. The move cost me my entire savings and the money I had saved up for the ring. In my mind, I had an expectation toward God that I was unaware of until this big move of faith felt like it was met with closed doors and disappointments. I thought God was going to meet my sacrifice with blessings and abundance, instantly to make up for the loss I had incurred. As it turns out, God's timing is a little different than ours. He is trying to develop something in us to become the person we are called to be. It began about a week before I had moved. There was a job that was set up for me when I was to arrive. A week before we moved, I found out the job fell through. I thought, *That's ok, God has something better for me! Right? If one door closes, another will open!* And within the first week, I got a job at a seafood restaurant. *Ok, this is going to be great!* I could feel the hope and excitement about this big risk paying off. Then the schedule came out and I was scheduled for four hours the first week. *Hmmm.* I remember thinking, *they must have done the schedule wrong. I got hired for a 28 hour a week job.* I talked to the manager and nothing changed. For six weeks I was only scheduled for four hours. After countless conversations to get more hours, I ended up forgetting about a two hour shift and was instantly fired. The thoughts came in like a flood. *Where is God? What is He doing? Does He not see my sacrifice? I gave everything to follow Him and nothing is working.* In this season I was elevating my own sacrifices, and experiences, above His nature. I was becoming a victim of my reality instead of surrendering the mystery and embracing His nature.

Now, this is easier said than done. Everything in me wanted to wallow in my self-pity and complain. And unfortunately at certain times during that season, I did. And every time I partnered with complaining I exalted my circumstances above the nature of God and tested Him just like Israel in the wilderness. As we take a look into Exodus we see that God displayed countless signs and wonders for the people of Israel to believe in Him. The list is pretty substantial; the ten plagues of egypt, His manifest Presence of a cloud by day and pillar of fire by night, manna coming down from heaven, water coming from a rock, bitter waters being made sweet, quail coming in the desert, and the list goes on and on. Miracles to display God's power, abundance, kindness, and nature, were received by an ungrateful people who had placed their circumstances and needs above the God they served. Many of us look at Israel and wonder how a people could complain in the midst of such a powerful supernatural environment, where God is showing up consistently. Yet, many of us find ourselves doing that very thing without realizing it. If I were to ask you right now what God has done in your life, would your answer be a past experience that lives in the past? Or would it be a past experience that created a present revelation and reality? We have to know and become aware of the God we want to belong to. He is a God who is constantly revealing His nature through the encounters and moments of breakthrough we have in our lives. Every encounter or breakthrough is an opportunity for us to get to know God better and to have a core revelation of Him instilled into our lives as a weapon for the next battle we are called to fight. **Life circumstances and situations are to lead us into a revelation of His nature through surrendering the mystery of what doesn't add up, to embrace the Truth of who He is.**

The Road of Revelation

When we see someone get healed we then get to decide whether it is going to become a moment in our history or a reality in our present. Every time God does something in our lives to reveal Himself it is an opportunity to discover His nature and a weapon in our lives. We see this revelation played out in John 14:13, "Whatever you ask in My name, that will I do, so that the Father may be glorified in the Son. If you ask Me anything in My name, I will do it." Jesus repeats this concept three more times. John 15:7 says, "If you abide in Me, and My words abide in you, ask whatever you wish, and it will be done for you," John 15:16, "You did not choose Me but I chose you, and appointed you that you would go and bear fruit, and that your fruit would remain, so that whatever you ask of the Father in My name He may give it to you." John 16:23-24 says, "In that day you will not question Me about anything. Truly, truly, I say to you, if you ask the Father for anything in My name, He will give it to you. Until now you have asked for nothing in My name; ask and you will receive, so that your joy may be made full." And the last time this is mentioned Jesus reveals an additional level of relationship and belonging that is possible as we step into this revelation of who God is. John 16:26-28 says, "In that day you will ask in My name, and I do not say to you that I will request of the Father on your behalf; for the Father Himself loves you, because you have loved Me and have believed that I came forth from the Father. I came forth from the Father and have come into the world; I am leaving the world again and going to the Father."

Jesus is making a declaration that is so incredible and is about to change the lives of His disciples who are hearing it, He repeats himself four times and then adds a fifth statement about it. This was the last time He is seen with His disciples before Judas betrays Him and Jesus thinks this concept is important to repeat. Why? Because it is a key to life and godliness, and getting back to the place of belonging in the Presence of God that Jesus was giving His life for. The disciples had a choice to realize everything they had seen Jesus do was a revelation of His nature and that they could confidently ask for anything within that nature and He would do it for them. "Ask anything in my Name." His names are Healer, Deliverer, Shepherd, God with us, Prince of Peace, Beginning and End, Almighty God, The God who Sees, The I Am, and the list goes on and on. **As we discover His name that reveals His nature, we confidently step into a realm of discovering our place of belonging in God.** This is not a passive stance, but a powerful revelation for those who believe according to His Name.

These verses reveal a vital part of our relationship with

God. When I discover my encounters with God, words He has spoken over me, and verses in the Bible that have spoken to me, all lead to a revelation of His true nature, I get an accurate picture of who God actually is. And when I discover who God actually is, I then can see who I am in Him. So then how does confidence come from belonging? When I discover the revelation of God's name which reveals His nature, I begin to realize I can ask for anything within that nature and it will be done for me. I start to partner with the higher calling of God in a place of confidence because I begin to see the God I want to belong to accurately. People that discover this reality are the ones Hebrews talks about "approach the throne of Grace with boldness."

One of the last conversations recorded before Judas betrays Jesus is this declaration. John 17:26, "and I have made Your name known to them, and will make it known, so that the love with which You loved Me may be in them, and I in them." Jesus has made the Father's name known to His disciples and the result of that revelation is His disciples receiving the same love that Jesus received from the Father—the love that was exemplified in the declaration, "This is my beloved Son. In whom I am well pleased." at the start of Jesus' journey.

We too can access this level of love and belonging. It all begins with surrendering the mysteries, situations, and unknown things to a loving, good, sovereign God. The opposite of surrender is control. Many people love to control aspects of their lives to provide a false sense of safety and stability that isn't real. The truth is that the control we think we have is an illusion. There are certain things I control in my life: my disciplines, structures, pursuits, and plans. But some of the bigger, scarier things, I realize I am not in control of. This has been a painful yet necessary lesson that I have had to learn and have helped many people, including Paisley, come to grips with. God is in control. Colossians 3:23-24 says "Whatever you do, do your work heartily, as for the Lord rather than for men, knowing that from the Lord you will receive the reward of the inheritance. It is the Lord Christ whom you serve." We must remember that we serve God, He doesn't serve us.

This can be a scary reality if we don't know the nature of the God, who is in control. If life feels crazy, and the thoughts of anxiety, loneliness, isolation, fear, pressure, performance, and control are in your head and feel like they are coming up, remember this promise in Romans 8:28, "God works all things out for good for those who love Him and are called according to His purpose." Amid broken humanity, painful realities, leadership wounds, and family dysfunctions, God is weaving a story together in our lives that if we hold onto Him and dive into the process and find Him, we will discover a story we are in awe of sharing. Your story and breakthrough will cultivate a greater sense of awe in God. The more you lean in, the more you will discover a Father who is so good at pursuing you, who is working all things out for your good.

Meditation Questions

1. Have my defining moments revealed God or caused me to question His nature?

2. Do I know the names of God by information or revelation?

3. Do I have head knowledge or heart awareness of who He is?

The Path Forward

1. Create space to write out painful defining moments and discover if an aspect of God's nature has been in question in your life since that moment? Next, remember good defining moments and encounters in your life and write down what aspects of God's nature were revealed to you from that moment?

2. Remember these areas of God's nature that have been in question. In chapter seven review what you have written to start the process of building truth again around His nature to dispel the questions. Remember God's nature is unchanging regardless of how circumstances play out on the earth.

Chapter 3:
What Does
Managing Pain
Look Like?

Pain is one of the universal realities that we as humans experience. While physical pain can make a person irritable, sensitive, and grumpy, our bodies are designed for it to heal over time. Emotional pain has a similar impact on a person's life, sometimes even greater, and yet emotional pain does not go away with time. Emotional pain in the form of disappointment, loss, betrayal, or rejection is something that most of us try to avoid by shoving painful experiences down into the depths of our emotional soul and then acting like it didn't happen or didn't hurt that bad. In this avoidance, we begin a more painful process of trying to manage our pain, which is the most accept-able form of self-abuse in our culture today. But is that the reality we have to live in? Is there a way for the burden of emotional pain to be healed, forgiven, and settled in a person's soul?

Sam's Story

Meet Sam, by 15 years old he had already been in drug rehab, was failing school, and was getting in heated fights with his parents that would lead to household objects be-ing thrown, move-out threats and calls to the police. You might be asking, "What happened in this young person's life to make this his 15-year-old reality? Was it his friends? Was it his parents? Was it the hand he was dealt in life? Did something bad happen to him that was unavoidable? While any one of these questions could lead us to a part of the answer, there was a greater reality of what was going on. Sam was in emotional pain and didn't know what to do with it. And emotional pain, if not healed, starts to leak out in different areas of our lives. It can force its way out through anger, partying, sexual activity, drugs, alcohol, anxiety, depression, fear, and the list goes on. In Sam's life, it forced its way out in ways that were ruining his life.

I had the privilege of meeting Sam right after he got out of rehab. Our first interaction was less than ideal. Forced by his parents to meet with a stranger, I knew this was going to be a difficult conversation. Once the initial conversation was over, which lasted all of 30 seconds, we proceeded to have one of the slowest-moving conversations of my life. It was filled with one-word answers or head nods from Sam, as we both struggled to try and get through this connect time. After that day I changed my gameplan with Sam as I realized that he didn't know how to talk about things in his life. Some people might look at that situation and say, "the person just wasn't open and ready to talk through the hard stuff." They might have even written Sam off as "not being worth their time." I saw through a different lens. One that came from my personal history. Pain and emotions were one of the hardest things to express in my life. I wasn't raised in a family where we had many talks around either of these topics, so I knew that for Sam opening up was going to take time.

Helping someone discover they are managing pain and it is doing more damage than the pain itself, is one of the hardest realities for a person to see. It takes a significant amount of trust and lots of space to begin the process of unlocking pain and emotions and getting the deep dark stuff of the soul out–the scary stuff that we wish no one would see, and even try to imagine doesn't exist. For Sam, this began with me slowly building trust with him and getting him to feel at ease around me. As a person feels like a person and not a project, their walls of self-protection and security start to come down. It took almost two years of building trust with this young man before he finally started to let me see him. I remember the day we were connecting as we sat on a bench and he took a deep breath and shared the beginning of the scariest things in his life. Things that had happened, things that had been said, things he had done. It took another nine to twelve months for Sam to fully open up to get the pain out.

Another View of a Foundational Story

There is a story in the Bible of a young man who allows poor perspectives to send him into a life of pain and sorrow. It is what happens in the story that reveals so much of what we can do when we are in pain, and what we can do if we are helping someone out of pain. We find it in Luke 15:11-32,

> And [Jesus] said, "A man had two sons. The younger of them said to his father, 'Father, give me the

share of the estate that falls to me.' So he divided his wealth between them. And not many days later, the younger son gathered everything together and went on a journey into a distant country, and there he squandered his estate with loose living. Now when he had spent everything, a severe famine occurred in that country, and he began to be impoverished. So he went and hired himself out to one of the citizens of that country, and he sent him into his fields to feed swine. And he would have gladly filled his stomach with the pods that the swine were eating, and no one was giving anything to him. But when he came to his senses, he said, 'How many of my father's hired men have more than enough bread, but I am dying here with hunger! I will get up and go to my father, and will say to him, "Father, I have sinned against heaven, and in your sight; I am no longer worthy to be called your son; make me as one of your hired men."' So he got up and came to his father. But while he was still a long way off, his father saw him and felt compassion for him, and ran and embraced him and kissed him. And the son said to him, 'Father, I have sinned against heaven and in your sight; I am no longer worthy to be called your son.' But the father said to his slaves, 'Quickly bring out the best robe and put it on him, and put a ring on his hand and sandals on his feet; and bring the fattened calf, kill it, and let us eat and celebrate; for this son of mine was dead and has come to life again; he was lost and has been found.' And they began to celebrate. "Now his older son was in the field, and when he came and approached the house, he heard music and dancing. And he summoned one of the servants and began inquiring what these things could be. And he said to him, 'Your brother has come, and your father has killed the fattened calf because he has received him back safe and sound.' But he became angry and was not willing to go in; and his father came out and began pleading with him. But he answered and said to his father, 'look! For so many years I have been serving you and I have never neglected a command of yours; and yet you have never given me a young goat, so that I might celebrate with my friends; but when this son of yours came, who has devoured your wealth with prostitutes, you killed the fattened calf for him.' And he said to him, 'Son, you have always been with me and all that is mine is yours. But we had to cele-brate and rejoice, for this brother of yours was dead and has begun to live, and was lost and has been found.'"

The younger son desires a life outside of what he is getting at home. While the Bible isn't clear on why, I can't help but imagine life at home wasn't all the son desired it to be. This is seen in the younger son taking his share of the inheritance, which signified that he was telling his father, "you are already dead to me." We then see that the younger son isn't launching to build a career, to steward his inheritance well, or even to start a family. We see indulgence, sin, and worldly pleasure filling his life. The full circle moment of how the son views home life is seen in his expectation of how his Father would accept him coming home. He imagines the bare minimum of a servant in the house. As we see in this story, pain can get us to have an altered view of society and the people around us. It creates a picture of life that isn't real, but in our own minds our perspective is the truth and it leads us to cope and try and fill the hole that pain creates.

Pain only leads a person in one direction–to the end of their ability. As depicted in the story above, the younger son finds himself poor, hungry, and on the verge of death; pain had led him to a place where he had to finally face it or choose to die. As he starts to recite his repentance, "I will get up and go to my father, and will say to him, 'Father, I have sinned against heaven, and in your sight; I am no longer worthy to be called your son; make me as one of your hired men,'" we can see part of the struggle of his pain. He believes his father is going to punish him. He has a poor perspective of his father that leads him to actual poverty. He prepares an analog to try and convince his dad to at least let him be a slave in his house. This story is an illustration of the Father being God, the older son being Israel, and the younger son being the Gentiles. Many of us live in pain, and disconnection because we have a view of God that makes us run when we are in pain instead of running to Him to have God heal our pain.

The True Gospel

This is part of the glorious gospel that many have watered down to becoming a ticket to heaven, instead of a new way of living on the earth. Jesus created a way for us to break cycles of pain and sin, so that we can become the very people that can carry Himself. Isaiah 53:5 prophecies of what Jesus would accomplish on the cross, "He was pierced for our transgressions, He was crushed for our iniquities, the chastening of our wellbeing fell upon Him, and by His scourging we were healed." The word "transgression" can be translated as "rebellion"[1], the word "inequities" is our guilt and punishment for things that were our fault.² The word "chastening" means "correction" or "discipline" and it is what gave us our wellbeing.³ And finally, "by his scourging" which translates as "stripes," "wounds," "we are healed."⁴ That word "healed" can be translated "to make whole."⁵ Jesus paid a price for us to step into wholeness. Many people stop at the punishment for sin and rebellion which he did take, and the weight of guilt and shame that he did destroy, but few talk about the wounds that made us whole. His body paid for us to be whole in our bodies, souls, and spirits. God made a way for us to become healed of pain, but like the younger son, many of us imagine the Father does not care about our whole lives: bodies, souls, and spirits. Many of us believe God only cares about getting our spirits into Heaven, when in reality He has made us His dwelling place. He cares deeply about how his house is doing.

As we look back on these two stories, Sam and the younger son, we can see all too often that people can walk around in so much pain and not even know it. Without the revelation of the pain we are carrying and a community of people discipling us out of pain, we as humans try to manage or avoid our pain. When we can't find a way out, or feel that there is no hope, we can get stuck in a pain cycle.

Pain Cycle Diagram

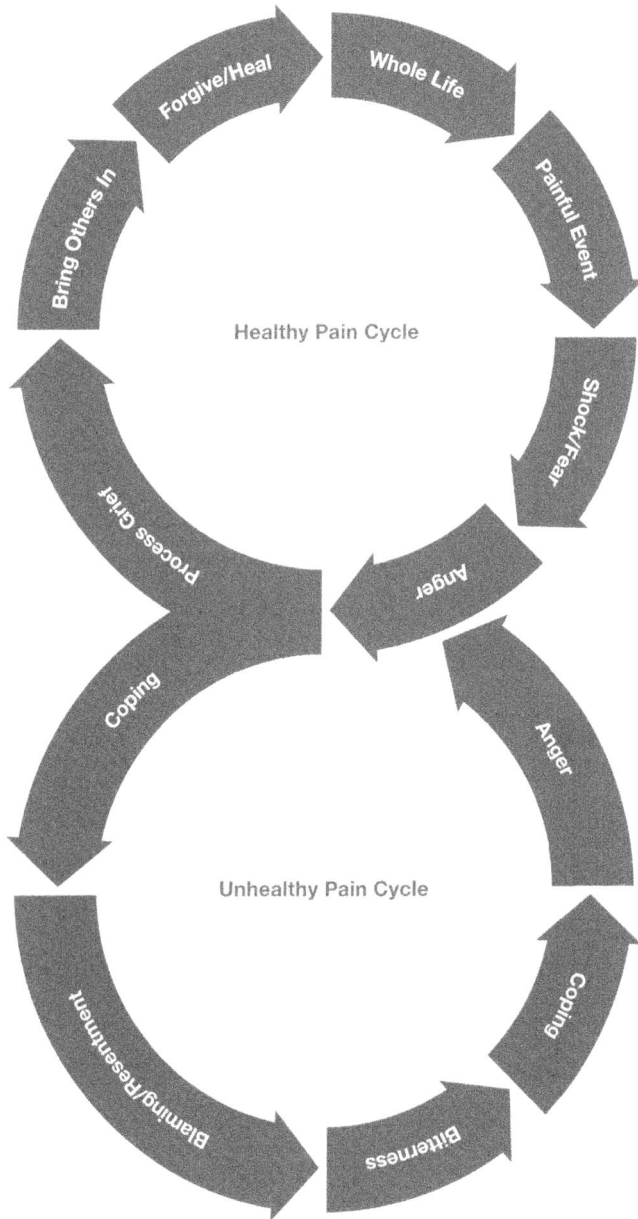

Healthy Pain Cycle:
Forgive/Heal → Whole Life → Painful Event → Shock/Fear → Anger → Process Grief → Bring Others In

Unhealthy Pain Cycle:
Anger → Coping → Bitterness → Blaming/Resentment → Coping

Unhealthy Pain Cycle

As we see in the Unhealthy Pain Cycle (refer to Pain Cycle Diagram on the previous page), without an understanding of the Father who gives grace that empowers us to walk in freedom and a plan, pain can lead to some scary places. Often, after the shock or fear of a painful event in our lives or a painful conversation has lifted, it leads us to anger. Paul exhorts the church of Ephesus by saying, "Be angry, and yet do not sin; do not let the sun go down on your anger, and do not give the devil an opportunity" (Ephesians 4:26-27). Anger is a natural response to painful events, though many people think anger is sin. I propose to you that anger is not sin, it is what you do with anger that will either set you up to heal and reconcile, or lead you to a place where the devil has an opportunity to lead you into places you do not want to go. If anger is left unchecked, it will lead a person into using coping mechanisms to overcome their intense feelings of anger. For many people this is the beginning of destructive sin cycles including pornography, excessive alcohol, drugs, checking out of the real world with technology, and other destructive coping mechanisms. As these cycles progress, they start to hurt other relationships in a person's life. As we saw with Sam, his pain was being taken out on his parents with rage, drugs and sexual sin cycles. What is even more intriguing is that as the anger led to these cycles, a victim mindset started to sink in that caused him to blame his parents and resent the world around him as if the world and everyone in it were causing him to behave the way he was. People who do not face their problems and have unresolved pain begin to blame others and resent the world. Because pain not dealt with leads people to become a victim.

Why? Because it is easier to blame someone else than take responsibility for something. Where this gets tricky in processing pain, is most times someone else caused us the pain, and therefore we are victims in the initial event, but many times people make that experience as a victim become an identity as a victim. This transition happens the moment the person decides they have no ability to overcome this pain because someone else has ruined their life. They wait for someone to say sorry, repair, or fix what they have done. In some cases the person who caused the pain is gone or the past event cannot be changed for whatever reason. These situations can lock a person up for fear of never being able to process the pain. They also reveal a deeper belief that pain is more power-ful than what God can heal. Pain is a real feeling and an intense feeling, but we get to decide, will it rule over us or will we overcome it?

The Unhealthy Pain Cycle (refer to Pain Cycle Diagram) continues with resentment turning into bitterness, which leads to deeper darker ways of coping. As mentioned earlier in this chapter, the cycle drives people into dark places with things that become unimaginable for humans to comprehend. The great lengths of sin that people engage in to try and overcome the pain they are feeling can eventually drive them into worlds of anxiety, depression, suicidal thoughts, loneliness, shame, and hardness of heart. As we discover this cycle, it gives us understanding and compassion for people who feel lost in darkness. What is the solution to all of the darkness and sin in the world? There is only one solution to it. There is only one way for a human being to change the cycle and step into the space of being a whole person again.

Healthy Pain Cycle

As we see in the Healthy Pain Cycle (refer to Pain Cycle Diagram), anger, when processed, and situations, when grieved, lead us to community, forgiveness, and ultimately wholeness. Processing pain also removes invisible weights that too many of us are carrying in our souls. These weights can become the hindrances to stepping into the full life that Jesus has paid for. But how can a person step into that choice? The first step is having the bench moment like Sam had, where he finally realized he was managing his pain rather than processing it, and it was destroying his life. It is the younger son coming to his senses. We must recognize that our destructive lifestyles are not a personality trait, or a product of being in the wrong place at the wrong time, or a sign of sin indulgence. For many of us, our destructive lifestyles are a symptom of trying to cope with the pain we are managing instead of facing it.

Over the next few chapters, we are going to break down the process of choosing to process pain instead of pushing down pain. We will discover what gives us the ability to grieve, and how to do it well. We will learn how to overcome resentment to get back to a place of wholeness, and ultimately how to forgive and find belonging with God and with people. As we go on this journey remember, in the right timing the Holy Spirit will bring up the pain that there is grace for you to overcome. We are not trying to deep dive into our problems, but we are asking the Holy Spirit if there is any unresolved pain that is causing problems and weights in our lives. A verse to remember as we step into the vulnerability and openness of processing pain is 1 John 1:6-9,

If we say that we have fellowship with Him and yet walk in the darkness, we lie and do not practice the truth; but if we walk in the Light as He Himself is in the Light we have fellowship with one another, and the blood of Jesus His Son cleanses us from all sin. If we say that we have no sin, we are deceiving ourselves and the truth is not in us. If we confess our sins, He is faithful and righteous to forgive us our sins and to cleanse us from all unrighteousness.

God is ready for us to come into the light with all our sins, pain, struggles, and fears so that we can have connection with one another again and feel his blood cleanse us so that we have fellowship with God our Father.

Meditation Questions

1. Holy Spirit, is there unresolved pain in my life?
2. Are signs of coping mechanisms showing up in my life?
3. If I were to be asked who I am angry with, who would it be?
4. Who has hurt me the most in my life? Have I faced that pain?

The Path Forward

1. Take time with the Holy Spirit and journal if any places of pain or situations came up while reading this chapter. Then ask the Holy Spirit if you have blamed people for situations in your life that feel as though they are unresolvable. Note: These will be the places we begin to walk the path of healing in, in the coming chapters.
2. Have a moment of honesty to discover if you have turned a moment of being victimized into an identity as a victim? Write truthfully what you are feeling as this is the process to releasing false identities and reclaiming the true identity and power over your life.

Chapter 4:
Facing Our Pain

Defining moments, both positive and negative, have
life-altering effects on our lives and facing these moments
are some of the most joyful and painful things a person
can do. Many people only want to think of the positive,
good experiences in life. They focus on the good, which is
amazing, but that can't be at the expense of denying the
bad. Many people live their lives believing the past is in
the past. While this is true, the effect of a past event can
live in the present if not dealt with. What I have learned in
my life is that a good defining moment builds faith, confidence, and trust in God that lasts far beyond the moment

and becomes a memory that I lean on in hard situations. Equally though, a painful negative defining moment pop ups as fear, anxiety, and paralysis when not dealt with. These moments cause our bodies to subconsciously protect ourselves from similar painful things moving forward. Pain is an unavoidable reality of life that, if not dealt with and faced, can alter a person's ability to connect, trust, and thrive in their relationships throughout their life. Facing pain with honesty, safety, and authenticity, opens up the door for healing to begin. Emotional pain is not healed over time, emotional pain is healed as we face it, expose it, and walk the road of forgiveness.

John 8:31-32 shares an intriguing point on the power of facing things in our lives. "So Jesus was saying to those Jews who had believed Him, "If you continue in My word, then you are truly disciples of Mine; and you will know the truth, and the truth will make you free." Another word for "truth" in this verse is "reality." If you will come to terms with reality, what is actually true, that reality will then create the place for authentic freedom to happen in your life.

While this verse brings truth, it also paves the way for questions many people have around pain. Do I need to talk about it? The past is in the past right? Burying things as if they never happened will make me forget about them. For me, the unprocessed pain that was caused by people had me living a life where people could not be trusted. Instead of facing the pain, I took on the belief that something was wrong with me and therefore I could and would never let anyone in. This way of thinking created deep rooted lies in my life of rejection, self-sabotage, and pain.

A Story of Pain

So what is the process of facing painful scenarios? Let me start by telling you a story. I was twelve years old and my family had recently moved to a new state. If you have ever done a move like this, you know that it takes some time to settle in and find your normal again. It took me about a year to feel that settling in, but then something happened that altered my life for many years. I was a gymnast, and had been going to a new gym for about six weeks. I felt like I was fitting in to the best of my ability, and honestly was enjoying it. The team was filled with all your average positions. The cool kid, the shy one, the new kid, the charismatic one, the silent group that is kind of mysterious but still cool, and then the kid that is unaware that most of the team didn't like him. No, I was not that kid.

I was in the new kid category still. One night in the middle of our practice, our entire team and head coach started to end practice and pack up before practice was over. I was a little confused and asked a team member what was going on. To my surprise one of the cool kids was having a sixteenth birthday party and had invited the whole gym including our coach, except for me, and to my dread, the other kid that no one liked. As I saw what was happening, the boy who was having the birthday came over to me and said, "Rory, I am sorry I didn't invite you, I just didn't feel like I knew you long enough to." I remember watching them all leave and as I turned around to see the assistant coach and that other kid with me alone in the gym, I saw in my mind's eye a neon sign flash above my head and it said, "loser". I went home that night and told my mom what happened. She did the most motherly thing anyone would do and said, "Rory you are not a loser." But something was different. My reality was no longer being shaped by my parents alone. To overcome the pain, I shoved the experience down as far as possible and acted like it didn't happen, and with that I started my new phase of life where making friends became really hard and social anxiety overtook me.

While everyone's journey is unique in what they go

through and how they face things, I do believe that certain things are common denominators in processing painful moments in a healthy way. The first step is to start to get honest with ourselves about certain painful moments and recognize how they have defined our beliefs in ourselves and in God. This sounds simple enough, but I have come to find that I would rather do anything else in the world than face a painful moment I have tried to forget. Why is that? Because something inside of me is afraid that what I am fearing about that moment could be true. Let me explain. After that kid didn't invite me to his birthday and I saw that sign over my head that said "loser", I struggled to tell anyone, besides my mom about that experience for years. The reason was that it had created such a blow to my foundation that was already faulty (I'll explain in a minute), and I was scared that what I experienced was true—that I was a loser. I believed that no one wanted to get to know me. And that I didn't belong in the group. Because of my fear that it could be true, I protected myself and others from ever seeing that memory or experience. Unfortunately, stuffing it down didn't get rid of the effects of what had happened. All it did was start the thread of many more reinforcing moments. My life became a reaction to the world around me. I was aware of every room I entered and who was in the room. I would measure myself against everyone,only talking to people I felt like I was equal with or better than. And with my low self-esteem, it meant I didn't talk to many people. I would avoid powerful guys in hallways at work, or if I was early to a meeting and noticed one or two other people in the room, out of fear of having to talk and connect I would awkwardly wait and be right on time to meetings to avoid connection. If I was about to go to the bathroom and noticed someone else going in that I was scared of talking to, I would walk to the other side of our offices just to avoid them. My life was crippled for years by this insecurity of who I was and a constant feeling that I wasn't enough.

The Past Affecting the Present

It wasn't until I was in my twenties and had a friend who was a counselor that helped me face this scary memory. At this time I was married, didn't have kids, and couldn't get close to anyone. I struggled opening up, being honest, hanging out, or even just connecting with people. My self-esteem was all wrapped up in what I did and how I led or served. The only way I could connect with anyone was if I was serving them or leading them. I went to her because I realized I didn't have any friends in my circle and wanted to know why. Boy was I not ready for the answers that would come. As I met with this girl she started the process of asking what I was so afraid of or why I struggle opening up to people. Now by this time, I had forgotten about that encounter as a twelve-year-old boy and all I could say was, I just don't trust people. She laughed, probed a little deeper, and asked, " Yes, but why? Has something happened to you around friendships that stops you?" I couldn't think of anything, and then a few days later I was in a morning prayer time with our staff. I was on my knees in worship and then, without warning I was transported in my mind back to this moment as a twelve-year-old boy at my gym, being rejected and picking up the label that I am a loser. And in an instant a wave of emotions hit me and I started crying–ugly crying. Ten-plus years of emotions that had been pent up were unleashed in a moment and my body physically was shaking as the pain of rejection and the fear that this might be true came flooding to the surface of my mind. I cried and cried as I started to replay the memory and the effects that it had had on my life. I also cried in fear because I knew I needed to tell someone about it and do the scariest thing, to let someone in on what had happened to me.

This decision was the start of breaking this stronghold in my life that hindered me from feeling like I belonged, from fully showing up in my life, and ultimately from being comfortable in my own skin and who God had made me to be. But to break a stronghold we first have to understand what it is. I like to describe a stronghold as a lie in our lives that we believe is true or partially true whether we are aware of it or not. Strongholds aren't just lies that we identify. If that were the case it would be easy to see them, because most of us can see lies we are believing. What makes them a stronghold is that something about that lie feels so true that we are afraid that we are being deceived to believe it is just a lie. If I know it's a lie then I don't have to believe it anymore. But if I am not confident it's not true, then it can control my life. They try to attach themselves to our identities. Many people have an "identity crisis" after painful moments in their lives. This was what was happening to me. I thought I was a loser and that no one would ever want to be my actual friend. I was scared that when I told someone what had happened to me, they would agree and validate the fear. And that was something I didn't think I could recover from.

That night after this encounter in staff prayer I started my journey of bravery and told my wife about the encounter I had had when I was twelve. I cried as she sat there and said, "Babe that isn't true." It was good to hear that, and

I knew I needed to tell more people to break the lie. The next person I told was my mentor, then our friend who was a counselor. I then took her advice and met up with a guy I had wanted to be friends with. I sat down and started the conversation in the most awkward way you could. I said, "Hey, I am really nervous being here and I am realizing I am not very good at making friends or letting people in, but I'd love to connect more with you and grow our friendship." Thankfully the guy welcomed me with open arms and became one of my closest friends in that season. The stronghold was being exposed and the more I stepped out, the more I started to see that what I was actually believing was a lie. I wasn't a loser. I wasn't bad at friendships. I had some negative defining moments that I needed to reveal, heal, forgive, and close in my life.

Reveal–
The process of exposing painful or scary scenarios, lies, or situations that we feel are holding us back from who we are called to be. It is the verse in 1 John 1:7, "But if we walk in the Light as He Himself is in the Light, we have fellowship with one another, and the blood of Jesus His Son cleanses us from all sin." Coming into the light to be seen is not just a matter of sin, but of every scary

thing we have hidden in darkness. As we bring our scary beliefs, situations, or moments, into the light we discover connection and fellowship again with people. Our ability to be vulnerable creates deeper fellowship and connection with one another, and the final reality of this verse is that the blood of Jesus covers these scary vulnerable and painful areas.

Heal–

Bringing the pain into the light creates the opportunity for the Holy Spirit to start the process of healing the wounds and revealing the truth about who you are and who He is. This process takes time and is not a momentary healing, but a gradual process of rooting out the lies that have shaped our lives and creating a space for truth to be found. In this process, we are renewing our minds to truth and tearing down the strongholds that have fortified themselves in our thinking.

Forgive–

Fully yielding my ability to change the past by accepting what has happened and choosing to forgive the debt of the offense without repayment. Once I could face and expose what had happened and realize that I was not what that kid had said, I was able to gain God's heart for him and forgive him. It took me a season to fully walk through forgiving him as I was made aware of how much this scenario had altered the course of my life. I had to forgive the kid and I had to forgive myself for letting this moment affect so much of my personality, life, and friendships.

Close–

The ability to fully walk through the pain cycle and remember the past without having any ongoing emotional effects from it. This is the ability to close a chapter or moment in a healthy way. Eventually I was able to close a chapter of my story, one that I am not ashamed of, scared of, in denial of, or bound by in my present reality. It is a chapter that has made me, me. As I look back on it, I am thankful for the breakthrough that has come in facing it.

Whatever the scenario, whatever the lie, God is ready to reveal His love and acceptance. See, this was only the beginning of my journey of unraveling the orphan mindset that rejected love at all cost so that I would be able to step into the Father's love as a son, fully belonging to Him. This was the start of me finding my place in the deep presence of God–His glory. This was the tip of the iceberg. I say this to help people not lose heart and not have a false finish line. We live in a quick-fix culture. I am as guilty as the next. So many things are at our fingertips that it is easy to believe that stuff can and should be dealt with efficiently. And if it is not then you must have something wrong with you. Oh wait there is that voice again, "Something is wrong with you. Why can't you overcome this quickly? Why are you still struggling? You faced that memory, didn't you? This isn't working. Nothing is working." And without us even realizing it we are back in the cycle.

The Woman in Pain
Luke 4:43-48 says,

> And a woman who had a hemorrhage for twelve years, and could not be healed by anyone, came up behind Him and touched the fringe of his cloak, and immediately her hemorrhage stopped. And Jesus said, "Who is the one who touched Me?" And while they were all denying it, Peter said, "Master, the people are crowding and pressing in on You." But Jesus said, "Someone did touch Me, for I was aware that

power had gone out of Me." When the woman saw that she had not escaped notice, she came trembling and fell down before Him, and declared in the presence of all the people the reason why she had touched Him, and how she had been immediately healed.

At first glance, this story seems to only be about physical healing, but some choice words would suggest that something else is being healed in this woman as well. From the first line, we see a woman who has been bleeding for twelve years, has tried everything but nothing has healed her. In the gospel of Mark 5:26 it says, "and [she] had endured much at the hands of many physicians, and had spent all that she had and was not helped at all, but rather had grown worse." Not only had this sickness stolen her wealth, but the desperation of a person whose disease is only getting worse also creates a sorrow of the soul. On top of this, there was an Old Testament reality still at play.

Leviticus 15:25-27,

> Now if a woman has a discharge of her blood many days, not at the period of her menstrual impurity, or if she has a discharge beyond that period, all the days of her impure discharge she shall continue as

though in her menstrual impurity; she is unclean. Any bed on which she lies all the days of her discharge shall be to her like her bed at menstruation; and everything on which she sits shall be unclean, like her uncleanness at that time. Likewise, whoever touches them shall be unclean and shall wash his clothes and bathe in water and be unclean until evening.

This verse exposes the deeper, more painful truth of what this woman was experiencing. She was considered unclean because of her condition which meant that everything and everyone she touched became unclean. Her condition set her up for rejection, isolation, and a lack of physical touch from the people around her. This desperation eventually leads her to risk it all. She would have been known in the community for being unclean and that is why she was most likely covered in garments to hide her identity in the crowd. She snuck through the crowd just to touch Jesus, knowing that if she touched Him, He would become unclean unless she was healed. This is why we read that she was "trembling" as Jesus tried to find who touched Him. She was about to come back into the community, reveal who she was and what had happened, and finally be freed from the torment of years of isolation and pain.

She had to overcome the identity of being unclean and an outcast in society to find the courage to go into a crowd to find Jesus. Many of us want healing, but we are scared to face the very things in our lives where we feel we don't belong, where we are unclean, and where we should hide. This story in the Bible reveals the possibility of what can happen when we bring our pain to Jesus and what He can do with it. Too many of us cling to the pain and make it our identity and in return convince ourselves that isolation is better than the fear of exposing our pain to the light. We forget the power of the Gospel and what Jesus accomplished on the cross.

Isaiah 53:3-5 says,

> He was despised and forsaken of men, a man of sorrows and acquainted with grief; and like one from whom men hide their face. He was despised, and we did not esteem Him. Surely our griefs He Himself bore, and our sorrows He carried; yet we ourselves esteemed Him stricken, smitten of God, and afflicted. But He was pierced through for our transgressions, He was crushed for our iniquities. The chastening of our well being fell upon Him, and by His scourging we are healed.

Isaiah shares how Jesus will know sorrow and grief, and will take our grief and sorrow upon Him so that in exchange we can be healed. Jesus didn't come to earth, die a gruesome death, and rise again just so we can go to heaven. He came so that He could bring heaven to the earth, and fully heal, restore, and redeem us from the life of sin, death, and pain we were living in. Many believers, though, never fully come to Jesus with the scary, embarrassing, painful things in our lives, and then we imagine God isn't powerful enough to heal us. The cross becomes a good notion, not a life-changing revelation. We become religious, nurturing our wounds and hiding our shame. We become the disjointed religious ones who have heard the Gospel but deny its power. Jesus came to redeem and restore our entire lives. Not just once, but throughout our lives. As painful things happen, He is there to redeem them. As people hurt us, He is there to restore. Our job is to bring things into the light where Jesus is so that we can be healed.

Breaking the Pain Cycle

The first step is taking the anger and pain and facing it instead of dismissing it. As we saw in the last chapter, if we dismiss it, it leads to a dark road of bitterness which

Pain Cycle Diagram

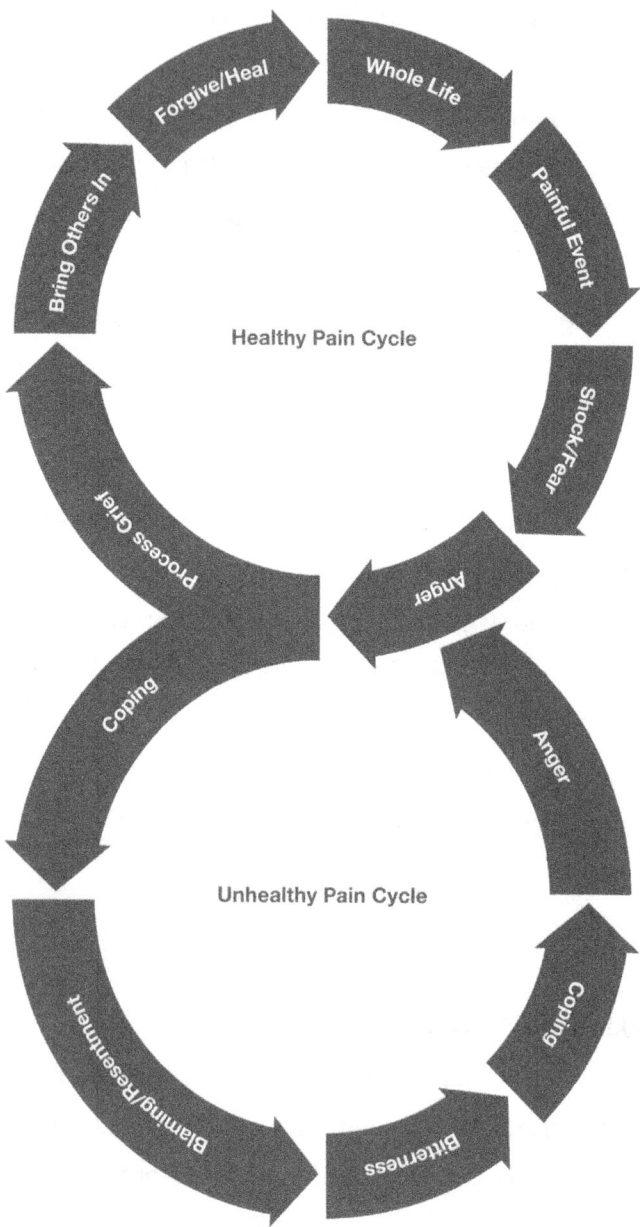

Healthy Pain Cycle

Forgive/Heal · Whole Life · Painful Event · Shock/Fear · Anger · Process Grief · Bring Others In

Unhealthy Pain Cycle

Anger · Coping · Bitterness · Blaming/Resentment · Coping

we will discuss next, but if we face it and allow the emotions of the pain to be felt and seen, it leads to the ability to process and grieve. Everytime there is pain, we have to process the effects of that pain in our lives and grieve what we have lost because of it. Remember Jesus knows our sorrows and grief. He is not stoic, He is present with us in our most painful moments. As we let Jesus and people in, we can start the 1 John process of coming back into fellowship and freedom.

The Next Step is Allowing Others In

This process has its challenges because we must overcome self-judgment and others' judgment of how we are feeling. Many people have a voice in their head saying, "You should be over this." I have found that anytime I hear the word "should" it is usually not the voice of God or the voice of a trusted friend. The voice of should almost always comes from the enemy to convince me to inflict self-judgment of where I am lacking or loosing, or others' judgment of how people are going to now see me. Unfortunately, many people in the church have become friends with the voice of shame and judgment and feel righteous in judging others for their worst days. This has led to many people being afraid to share their scary moments or things that they haven't been able to overcome because of the judgment. I also believe this is why counselors and therapists have replaced leaders and discipleship. People need others to help them overcome pain, but too many people in the church have let judgment overcome mercy. They haven't faced their own pain, and in return aren't able to help those who are in pain. They end up rejecting pain in others because they have rejected facing the pain in themselves. This is fascinating when even in the Bible, James 2:13 declares, "For judgment will be merciless to one who has shown no mercy; mercy triumphs over judgment." We have lost something pivotal in a person's process of finding their place in God's presence. How do we walk in the light with Jesus when we have others who don't allow us to bring our dark areas into the light to be healed?

The Church's Call

The church is to be known as a place of healing and freedom, but sadly it is often known as a place of judgment and hypocrisy. For many our hypocrisy is a byproduct of the fear of letting people see us because of the fear of others' judgment. Jesus declared why He came, and what His Spirit would do on the earth. As Luke 5: 29-32 describes,

And Levi gave a big reception for Him in his house; and there was a great crowd of tax collectors and other people who were reclining at the table with them. The Pharisees and their scribes began grumbling at His disciples, saying, "Why do you eat and drink with the tax collectors and sinners?" And Jesus answered and said to them, "It is not those who are well who need a physician, but those who are sick. I have not come to call the righteous but sinners to repentance."

And Paul writes in 2 Corinthians 3:17, "Now the Lord is the Spirit, and where the Spirit of the Lord is, there is liberty." Jesus' heart is to free people and heal people. He gave his very life to set people free, and yet many have missed the healing power of Jesus working in their lives because of judgment from themselves or others.

Overcoming the Fear of Judgment

To overcome something, one first must understand what that something is. The fear of judgment is played out in two distinct ways in our lives. The first is self-judgment. Self-judgment is the fear that what I have done or the pain I have endured is now a part of my identity. I can no longer heal or overcome it because it is actually who I am and in that belief, I have cast judgment on myself and bound myself to the very lie or pain that is destroying me. It is the person whose parents underwent a divorce who is convinced they were the reason their parents separated. The painful event led to a belief that they are the destructive one who destroys relationships. Now most of us would know that is not true, but to the one who is held in self-judgment, that is the truest reality they can grab onto. It is also the place where Jesus wants to set them free.

The second is others' judgment, which is the fear that people will disassociate from me or think less of me when I let them in on my worst days and my darkest thoughts. The fear of what others think and what others may do when they discover my pain leads many to never share it. Unfortunately, this is confirmed by how many people in the church respond to someone's worst day. Instead of being like Jesus, who was continually in the midst of unclean, hurting and broken people, we have created a false sense of freedom through performance, hiding, and playing church. Many of us have experienced a culture of judgment and punishment in a church and among believers. We must return to the Gospel Jesus preached and revealed. The true Gospel transforms, heals, and frees.

Any other gospel that doesn't produce this in a person's life isn't the Gospel at all.

What could happen to a person if they are met with mercy on their worst day? There was a young man that I was mentoring who confessed he was messing around with a girl who wasn't his girlfriend. I'll let you fill in the blank. The young man was visibly terrified and could barely look at me as he shared with me what had been happening the past two weeks. I was the first person he had told. Once he was finished telling me I had him look at me, and I said, "I am so proud of you for letting me know." I walked over to the couch he was sitting on, sat next to him, and hugged him as he started weeping. Confession wasn't going to heal this young man, but it was the start. **In the scariest moment of coming into the light, a person needs to be met with mercy, compassion, and covering.** It doesn't mean we don't have things to figure out, it means I am for you and love you.

Something I have learned on the journey of overcoming my own pain and helping others face and overcome theirs is realizing that poor decisions and coping destructive behaviors are driven by pain. Many of us get locked into poor behavior, instead of realizing it is revealing pain that has never been exposed. Did the young man still have a mess to clean up and sin to repent of? Yes. Were there more things to be discovered that were painful? Yes. How I reacted to the mess was going to determine if he would show me his heart. The heart is the place of transformation, not behavior. Too many leaders, parents, and people try to manage behavior and never access hearts, the true place of transformation. In this process of opening up, you need to find a leader who bears the fruit of mercy and validates the pain without forgetting the transformational power of the gospel. Validating pain doesn't mean allowing someone to become a victim. Validating pain allows a person to feel what they have been trying to hide for years, realizing that facing it is better than imagining it never happened. Mercy that leads to repeated cycles of sin or pain isn't mercy. Mercy that leads to the redeeming power of Jesus that heals, restores, and redeems is the place you want to find yourself. This young man over the next several months started the journey with me of letting me see every scary, painful thing that had happened in his life. As he faced things, cried, yelled, grieved, shared, and forgave each painful moment, he started getting his life back. Jesus was healing and transforming his heart.

Mercy Triumphs Over Judgment

It reminds me of the story in John 8:1-11,

> But Jesus went to the Mount of Olives. Early in the morning He came again into the temple, and all the people were coming to him; and He sat down and began to teach them. The scribes and the Pharisees brought a woman caught in adultery, and having set her in the center of the court, they said to Him, "Teacher, this woman has been caught in adultery, in the very act. Now in the Law Moses commanded us to stone such women; what then do you say?" They were saying this, testing Him, so that they might have grounds for accusing Him. But Jesus stooped down and with His finger wrote on the ground. But when they persisted in asking Him, He straightened up, and said to them, "He who is without sin among you, let him be the first to throw a stone at her." Again He stooped down and wrote on the ground. When they heard it, they began to go out one by one, beginning with the older ones, and he was left alone, and the woman, where she was, in the center of the court. Straightening up, Jesus said to her, "Woman, where are they? Did no one condemn you?" She said, "No one, Lord." And Jesus

said, "I do not condemn you, either. Go. From now on sin no more."

Jesus reveals the heart of mercy, with grace to be transformed. He shows her mercy and covers her in her shame, weakness, sin, and pain, and then releases grace to go and sin no more. This gave her the ability to overcome her hardest day, to step back into society, and to overcome. We will be on both sides of this situation in our lives. There will be times when we are the ones opening up about painful moments in our lives, and other times when people will open up to us. Our job is to gain the right understanding of pain and healing through Jesus so that whatever season we are in we know how to run in and process pain because we know that it leads to healing and freedom.

Pain is a part of all of our lives. How we face pain and walk through it determines the level of wholeness and freedom we walk in as believers. Instead of trying to avoid it, let's discover the grace-filled power of God to overcome it and be healed of it. As I have gone through this process of facing pain, allowing Jesus to heal areas in my life that I never thought could be healed, it has opened me up to a level of wholeness and confidence I never thought was possible. I went from being the socially awkward loser kid to a whole and confident man. This confidence can only be found in the Gospel of Jesus. He took on our sin, pain, sorrow, grief, loss, and struggle, to give us a new and thriving life in Him. In the next chapter, we will look at what happens if we choose to isolate and not let others in.

Meditation Questions

1. What Pain am I avoiding looking at?
2. What fear is gripping me from letting someone into that pain?
3. Do I believe I am my greatest fears?

The Path Forward

1. Take a moment to journal the answers to these questions above. Create a safe space to let a leader or a friend into this place of pain and fear. The goal is not to have them fix anything, but to have someone hear you. Set them up for success by setting up that expectation when you meet with them.
2. What lie are you believing about yourself, regarding your greatest fear? Once you write down the lie, take a moment to hear the Holy Spirit speak the truth of how He sees you. If you have a hard time hearing, find a trusted friend or leader to let into this lie that has wrapped around your identity for them to speak the truth over you.

Chapter 5:
The Two Roads
Traveled

"Why did God let this happen?" "Why would a loving God not stop that person from hurting me?" "Why didn't God protect me from that person?" "Is God safe?" These are the type of questions that can come up for believers in the face of painful situations. Many of the questions we ask don't have a clear or easy answer. So what do you do if you are navigating the hard questions? With any painful situation, the road we choose to walk down is a choice. We can choose forgiveness or resentment. Unfortunately, we can't have both. The question that causes many to decide which road they will travel down is simple in nature and profound to answer: "Why did God let that painful thing happen to me?" This is a very personal question that myself and many believers have had to come face to face with in our walk with God. It is an important question to ask, but even more important is the road we take to discover the answer. We will find ourselves either on a road that leads to resentment towards God and unbelief, or one that leads us to a powerful reality of the nature of God even if that nature is found in mystery.

The Road of Resentment

Resentment is the feeling a person has when they blame someone else for their life and pain and it sets a person up to walk in unforgiveness. For many people, behind a painful experience is lurking resentment or offense that if not dealt with can turn to hatred. The road of resentment is the path toward unforgiveness and hatred and many people walk on it to avoid facing the scary things in their lives. We as humans would rather blame the person who committed the offense that caused the pain and justify an offense instead of facing the reality of the pain. Facing pain doesn't heal it, but it does allow us to finally see it for what it is. Resentment is a road that many believers have walked down that leaves them more lost than found, disillusioned instead of healed, and exposed to torment from the enemy instead of covered by God.

Pain that doesn't lead us to vulnerability with people, will lead us to cope in a fantasy world. As we see in the pain cycle, the step of anger will either lead us to people or towards a coping mechanism. Many addictions start in a person's life after a painful moment or event has taken place. Trauma, if not healed, leads to uncontrollable addictive cycles, as a human tries to cope with the pain they are feeling inside. Many attempt to use these coping devices to check out of reality and dull the festering pain. This is why many people find themselves drinking too much alcohol, doing drugs, binge-watching TV, scrolling on social media endlessly, engaging in sexual activities like porn and masturbation, and the list goes on. As this reality sinks in, we can look around the earth and see that a lot of people are in pain because a lot of people use these vices to check out of reality. We have to remember Jesus' words in John 8:31 where He says, "If you continue in My word, then you are truly disciples of Mine; and you will know the truth and the truth will make you free." Pain tries to get us to check out while truth keeps us in reality and in our present reality of truth we see clearly. Fantasy is when our lives begin to feel like a fog and our purpose feels nowhere to be found. This is how people in pain can do wicked, destructive things that hurt the people they love, and can convince themselves it doesn't matter. They are living in a fog or a dream, and are not in reality.

The cycle progresses from coping to blaming and onto resentment. Instead of facing the pain that is causing us to try and escape through different vices, we begin to blame the person, situation, institution, leader, church, job or parent and in the process of blaming, we form an offense that leads to resentment. As we form our case, justifying our indignation, offense, and our right to be hurt and mad, we form the foundation for unforgiveness that settles in our hearts. The human heart was not created to carry unforgiveness. It leads us down the road of anger, coping, sin, and demonic oppression. Unforgiveness is one of the few things that opens doors in our lives to the demonic realm. When the door is open, they have access to mess with us. Many people who carry the burden of unforgiveness can experience mental health issues, anxiety, unhealthy coping habits, isolation, and a victim outlook on life. These are effects of an open door into the spirit realm.

Is the House Secure?

Whenever we have unforgiveness in our lives it is similar to leaving the front door of our soul open. In life, if you were to leave your front door open it may be okay for a little while, but you never know the day someone could walk past and seize the opportunity to break into your house. In the same way, unforgiveness opens a door in our lives where the demonic realm has access to steal and torment us in different ways. Even science has found that there are physical effects of unforgiveness on the human body. The negative health effects of unforgiveness are widely documented and include but are not limited to stress, increased depression and anxiety, social isolation, and even compromised physical health due to stress on one's immune system.[1] The stress in our bodies increases as we carry the burden of what someone else has done to us. Even in the pain cycle that we have walked through, scientists say "unforgiveness may be the state in which the anger that the victim experiences takes hold of their daily lives, eventually impacting their overall well-being."[2] This is why anger is the pivotal step in the cycle either toward healing or toward coping and more pain. Anger will either become our everyday normal experience, or we can process it with people and find openness, wholeness, and a sense of purpose again in our lives.

When we feel wronged and in pain because of someone's actions, the process of dealing with that pain will either stiffen you or launch you. The temptation many times in seasons of walking through varying degrees of pain is to try to rationalize the pain to subdue its impact and push it down, instead of staring at the pain and seeing it healed. Pain is a tricky thing because it can have the appearance of a dark mountain that looms over your life, making you feel powerless, lost, and overwhelmed with where to start the treacherous climb to overcome it.

In reality, pain is just that...it's painful. Humans are also really good at doing whatever it takes to avoid pain. Why? Because it's painful! When the pain is not expressed it is impossible to truly forgive someone. Unforgiveness is the first step on the road of resentment that leads to unbelief, and eventually a hardness of heart. For years I was unable to process my pain because I was so shut down emotionally due to the many defining moments of pain that built up over the years. I felt overwhelmed with where to start. I had to realize that there were steps to this that would unlock who I was. It was a process guided by my Father who was leading me back to the place of belonging. Back to the place where I am fully loved, fully accepted, and fully free in His Presence.

Our Home in His Presence

This is not some euphoric place, but a reality for every person who believes in Jesus and has made Him Lord. Jesus shares this reality by saying in John 14:1-5,

> "Do not let your heart be troubled; believe in God, believe also in Me. In my Father's house are many dwelling places; if it were not so, I would have told you; for I am going to prepare a place for you. If I go and prepare a place for you, I will come again and receive you to Myself, that where I am, there you may be also. And you know the way where I am going." Thomas said to Him, "Lord, we do not know where you are going, how do we know the way?" Jesus said to him, "I am the Way, and the Truth, and the Life; no one comes to the Father but through Me."

Jesus has created this place of belonging. It was one of the main reasons He came to the earth–to reconcile humanity back to the Father and to restore us back to perfect union and connection with God. He came to allow every soul to find true fulfillment and belonging in the presence of a Father.

How do we navigate the "why" questions listed at the beginning of this chapter? We have to go back to how God created the earth and how He set up humanity. In Genesis 1:27 "God created man in His own image, in the image of God He created him; male and female He created them." Then in the next chapter, Genesis 2:7-9 it says,

> Then the Lord God formed man of dust from the ground, and breathed into his nostrils the breath of life; and man became a living being. The Lord God planted a garden toward the east, in Eden; and there He placed the man whom He had formed. Out of the ground the Lord God caused to grow every tree that is pleasing to the sight and good for food; the tree of life also in the midst of the garden, and the tree of the knowledge of good and evil.

Then in verse 2:15-17,

> Then the Lord God took the man and put him into the garden of Eden to cultivate it and keep it. The Lord God commanded the man, saying, "From any tree of the garden you may eat freely; but from the tree of the knowledge of good and evil you shall not eat, for in the day that you eat from it you will surely die."

The Bible continues in Genesis 3:1-7,

> Now the serpent was more crafty than any beast of
> the field which the Lord God had made. And he said
> to the women, "Indeed, had God said, 'you shall not
> eat from any tree of the garden?'" The woman said to
> the serpent, "From the fruit of the trees of the garden
> we may eat; but from the fruit of the tree which is in
> the middle of the garden, God has said, 'you shall
> not eat from it or touch it, or you will die.'" The ser-
> pent said to the woman, "You surely will not die! For
> God knows that in the day you eat from it your eyes
> will be opened, and you will be like God, knowing
> good and evil." When the woman saw that the tree
> was good for food, and that it was a delight to the
> eyes, and that the tree was desirable to make one
> wise, she took from its fruit and ate; and she gave
> also to her husband with her, and he ate.

Free Will

The first thing we must discover on our journey to why
painful things happen is to understand free will. God
created the earth and humanity and all that is on the earth.
He then took man and woman and placed them in the

Garden of Eden where there were two trees to give the man and woman a choice. They could choose to obey what God had said or they could choose to disobey and obey another's voice. Why would God do something like that? The earth is massive. Place the trees in some forbidden cave that is impossible to get to that no one would discover, right? We all love the idea of freedom, and not being controlled until someone uses their freedom to hurt us. Then we want to know why people aren't controlled. Without the choice for humans to choose good or evil, God would not be a loving Father. He would be a controlling leader. The very nature of choice creates the ability for people to walk in freedom or choose to harm someone. The foundation of the world was built on humans' ability to choose. Many of us want God to grant us freedom, and control everyone else who would cause us pain. In our own minds, we can wish to be the center of the universe. Only good happens to me and everyone who is bad is controlled and stopped. Unfortunately, that isn't how God set up the world. He wants people to have a choice to love Him and love one another. Without free will and the ability to feel pain, we also wouldn't have the ability to love.

In Genesis 1:28-30 it says,

> God blessed them; and God said to them, "Be fruitful
> and multiply, and fill the earth, and subdue it; and
> rule over the fish of the sea and over the birds of the
> sky and over every living thing that moves on the
> earth." Then God said, "Behold, I have given you
> every plant yielding seed that is on the surface of
> all the earth, and every tree which has fruit yielding
> seed; it shall be food for you; and to every beast of
> the earth and to every bird of the sky and to every
> that that moves on the earth which has life, I have
> given every green plant for food", and it was so.

When we stop and let this reality sink in that God gave
man free will and He even went a step further by giving us
authority over the whole earth. We realize that God intend-
ed for man to rule over the earth and to create a culture
and environment for humanity to thrive in. He gave us all
the essentials and then placed them in our hands. When
we hear this part of the story of what God started with and
what He gave us, it is easy to believe that God is good!
But when I look at life and reality around me, that thought
quickly changes to more questions than realities. Why?
Because people's free will has allowed choices of sin and

pain to enter the world. This is the tension of every believer, a loving God gives us choice and free will, which in turn allows sin and pain to be in the world. Without free will there would be no sin, but there would also be no choice to love. This beautiful and painful reality gives the responsibility of humanity back to humanity. What I mean by that is that we are responsible for stewarding the Earth, the relationships on the Earth, the people and creatures on the Earth, and part of that stewardship is forgiving when people hurt us and wrong us. God isn't making the world bad, and it technically isn't God's responsibility to change the world, because He has given authority to men and women to rule and reign over the earth. Too many believers are waiting to get rescued from the Earth, instead of stepping into their rightful authority to rule on the Earth.

How Do We Get Off the Road of Resentment?

There is a beautiful parable in John 7:36-50 where Jesus reveals how to overcome resentment and unforgiveness.

> Now one of the Pharisees was requesting Him to dine with him, and He entered the Pharisees house and reclined at the table. And there was a woman in the city who was a sinner; and when she learned

that He was reclining at the table in the Pharisee's house, she brought an alabaster vial of perfume, and standing behind Him at His feet, weeping, she began to wet His feet with her tears, and kept wiping them with the hair of her head, and kissing His feet and anointing them with the perfume. Now when the Pharisee who had invited Him saw this, he said to himself, "If this man were a prophet He would know who and what sort of person this woman is who is touching Him, that she is a sinner." And Jesus answered him, "Simon, I have something to say to you." And he replied, "Say it, Teacher." "A moneylender had two debtors: one owed five hundred denarii, and the other fifty. When they were unable to repay, he graciously forgave them both. So which of them will love him more?" Simon answered and said, "I suppose the one whom he forgave more." And He said to him, "You have judged correctly." Turning toward the woman, He said to Simon, "Do you see this woman? I entered your house; you gave Me no water for My feet, but she has wet My feet with her tears and wiped them with her hair. You gave Me no kiss; but she, since the time I came in, has not ceased to kiss My feet. You did not anoint My head with oil, but she anointed My feet with perfume. For this reason

I say to you, her sins, which are many, have been forgiven, for she loved much; but he who is forgiven little, loves little." Those reclining at the table with Him began to say to themselves, "Who is this man who even forgives sins?" And He said to the woman, "Your faith has saved you; go in peace."

In this story, we see Jesus reveal a kingdom reality that empowers us to gain the proper perspective of situations that can be painful, ugly, or scary. He then goes on to describe how this proper perspective not only sets us up to be saved and find peace but empowers us to love people well. We can even love people that we find unlovable in our lives because of the pain they have caused us. How is this possible? How can we get off the road of resentment? In this parable, Jesus reveals two people who owed debts to the same moneylender. The moneylender graciously forgave both debts, but one debt was bigger than the other. Jesus asks Simon, the Pharisee (a Jewish religious teacher of the day), which of the men forgiven of their debt would love more. Simon shares how the one whose debt to pay was greater would love more. This story can seem offensive. The people who have done lots of bad things and who need a lot of forgiveness learn to love more. For years I remember thinking that this story was unjust and would get angry when I would read it. Do I need to go and do bad things and hurt people to learn how to love? Or do I need a lot of painful things to happen to me so that I have to forgive people a lot to learn how to love? That seems cruel.

I was understanding this verse from a me-centered reality. I was placing my own works and my own forgiveness as the baseline to understand the meaning. When we do this, we miss much of what the Bible is saying. The Bible is not a me-centered book where I become the main character of every story. It is a book revealing Jesus the son of God and His story of saving and healing humanity. The moment I realized Jesus was the champion of this story, I understood what this parable was all about. Every person is in debt to God for the sin we have been born into or have engaged with. Romans 6:23 says, "For the wages of sin is death, but the free gift of God is eternal life in Christ Jesus our Lord." Sin has cost us life. Because Eve and Adam disobeyed God and obeyed the devil, sin reigned supreme. The cost of that sin is death for every individual. We see this same reality in the Old Testament where Ezekial hears the word of the Lord in Ezekiel 18:20, "The person who sins will die. The son will not bear the punishment for the Father's iniquity, nor will the father bear the punishment for the son's iniquity; the righteousness of the righteous will be upon himself, and the wickedness of the wicked will be upon himself." These verses are two of many examples where sin leads to death, and the cost of sin is death. This is the power of what Christ has done through the cross. We will talk more in the next chapter of what fully took place, but for the sake of getting off the road of resentment, we must understand that our sin was too great and Christ chose to forgive us.

As we look back at the parable of the money lender that had two debtors, the person who realizes what great forgiveness they have received from Christ for the debt of sin that is impossible to repay has the ability to love. The ability to love in the midst of pain is the way people can get off the road of resentment. When we are aware of the great forgiveness we have received through the cross, it puts into perspective the debt of pain we have to forgive from someone who hurt us. We will talk in the next chapter how we walk through the process of forgiving someone who has hurt us. But the first step is discovering our own debt of sin that has been freely forgiven. **The greater the reality of the cross in our lives the greater our ability to forgive. The greater the revelation of Christ's finished work in our lives, the greater our ability to live in love.**

As we embrace the mystery of painful moments and things we cannot control, and lean into who God is we must follow Christ's example. 1 Peter 2:21-24 says,

> For you have been called for this purpose, since Christ also suffered for you, leaving you an example for you to follow in His steps, who committed no sin, nor was any deceit found in his mouth; and while being reviled, He did not revile in return; while suffering, He uttered no threats, but kept entrusting Himself to Him who judges righteously; and He Himself bore our sins in His body on the cross, so that we might die to sin and live to righteousness; for by His wounds you were healed.

In this verse we see that Christ suffered and had people revile him. That word means to, "criticize in an abusive or angrily insulting manner."[3] While being criticized and angrily insulted he didn't retaliate, because he trusted the nature of God. Our ability to forgive and step off the road of resentment is to trust in the nature of God and His ability to judge righteously and make things work out for the good that doesn't seem good at all. He can take our hardest moment and most painful season in life and bring healing, restoration, and forgiveness. While He won't control how others respond, because that would go against His nature to give free will, He can walk a person into complete healing and freedom from any painful moment or season in their life. Pain and unforgiveness try to steal hope, but remember He is "the God of hope [that] fill[s] you with all joy and peace in believing so that you will abound in hope by the power of the Holy Spirit" (Romans 15:13).

Meditation Questions

1. How have I handled anger? Do I blow up, shut down, avoid, or punish the person who hurt me?

2. Do I understand my own free will? Do I use my own choices to love and forgive or do I expect others to do what I am not willing to do?

The Path Forward

1. Take a moment to journal to discover if you have allowed resentment or unforgiveness from painful situations to remain in your life? As memories or people come to mind, journal the feelings and impact that these people have had on your life. This is the first step to processing anger in a healthy way. Facing the pain and allowing the anger out through journaling, gives your heart permission to feel the deep feelings that are sometimes hard to say out loud.

2. Take time this week to go and do something fun that refreshes you. As we face pain, it is important that we continue to do fun things, see people, and live life. The goal is not to deep dive into pain and isolation, but to live life learning how to process pain effectively that leads to healing.

Chapter 6:
Forgiveness
and All Its Perks

He sat on the couch in my office. The windows allowed a warm light into the room. The surroundings felt serene, but the young man on my couch was in turmoil. Hunched over in silent agony with only his shoulders moving to reveal the deep sobs he was releasing. I sat there quietly, waiting, giving him the space to share the painful things that had happened in his life that the world had never known about. Minutes passed that seemed like hours as a quivering voice tried to get out what had happened to him in his past and things he had done that he never wanted anyone to know about–things that had haunted him into his present. As I listened, intentionally silent, not moving, I gave him permission to be fully seen. He was laying his soul bare before me and getting the pain out. The tension turned into relief the more he shared. And the lightness of his soul through vulnerability gave way for forgiveness to become his reality. This moment led him to begin the process of forgiveness.

True Forgiveness

What is true forgiveness? Is it in the words? Some would like to imagine it is. We were raised to quickly say sorry and then the person would have to respond, "I forgive you." Did they really? Is this the exchange that sets someone free? Many want to believe it is. They want to forget about the pain and move on as quickly as possible so that they can stop thinking about it. Forgiveness though is so much more than just words or forgetfulness, it is intentional and something every believer has the responsibility to walk in while on the earth. It is the process of releasing a person who has harmed you, violated you, or hurt you from the expectation of fixing the offense, changing their behavior, or cleaning up their mistake. You might be wondering, *Rory, am I supposed to forgive someone who isn't changing?* Before you stop reading, you might find that my answer will lead you down a road of becoming a powerful person again in a situation that makes you feel powerless. Yes, it is our responsibility to forgive a person regardless of if they change, repent, or apologize.

If forgiveness is dictated by the response of the person who committed the wrong then we will be bound by someone else's free will. Let me paint a scenario to explain this. If you, like so many others, have had one of your parents walk out on your family while you were young, then you are aware of pain and mess that feels unsolvable. In these more permanent situations, like a divorce, that separates a family for good, how can someone forgive if the mess can't be cleaned up and fixed? If the only way to forgive is if the person who causes the pain cleans it up, then most people would be bound to a life of unforgiveness and bitterness. People that cause us pain sometimes never repent, apologize or change. When we think forgiveness is found in the change, we set ourselves up to have our emotions and life controlled by the decisions of someone else.

Benefits of Forgiveness

Even scientists are discovering the effects of forgiveness

on a person's body. In a study on forgiveness they found it is, "a way to resolve anger (and other transgression-related negative emotions) which in turn leads to various psychological and physical health benefits" the most prominent of those side effects is that "forgiveness is a way to restore hope for the future."[1] This reminds me of a famous verse in the bible Jeremiah 29:11. "For I know the plans that I have for you, declares the Lord, plans for welfare and not for calamity to give you a future and a hope." This declaration from the Lord is in the midst of a time when the nation of Israel is in captivity in Babylon. They were suffering and in pain, and yet God revealed something profound–that He wanted to give them a hope and a future. How do we access those things? By walking in forgiveness towards the people who have unjustly hurt us and caused us pain who might never change. The study also found that "forgiveness interventions have shown such an effect of forgiveness on both reduced anger and increasing hope among other outcome variables such as anxiety, depression, and self-esteem." Believers often hear "forgiveness" and feel it is unjust, yet God understands the implications on your life and future when you choose to forgive. Forgiveness is a choice and one that sets a believer up to access good things in their future regardless of the pain in their past.

Seventy Times Seven

How do we cultivate a lifestyle of forgiveness? How do we navigate the pain cycle well and walk the road of wholeness in the midst of painful scenarios. There is a story in Matthew 18:21-35 that reveals the perspective we need to walk in for a lifestyle of forgiveness:

> Then Peter came and said to Him, "Lord, how often shall my brother sin against me and I forgive him? Up to seven times?" Jesus said to him, "I do not say to you, up to seven times, but up to seventy times seven. For this reason the Kingdom of heaven may be compared to a king who wished to settle accounts with his slaves. When he had begun to settle them, one who owed him ten thousand talents was brought to him. But since he did not have the means to repay, his lord commanded him to be sold, along with his wife and children and all that he had, and repayment to be made. So the slave fell to the ground and prostrated himself before him, saying, 'Have patience with me and I will repay you everything.' And the lord of that slave felt compassion and released him and forgave him the debt. But that slave went

out and found one of his fellow slaves who owed him a hundred denarii; and he seized him and began to choke him, saying, 'Pay back what you owe,' So his fellow slave fell to the ground and began to plead with him, saying, 'Have patience with me and I will repay you.' But he was unwilling and went and threw him in prison until he should pay back what was owed. So when his fellow slaves saw what had happened, they were deeply grieved and came and reported to their lord all that had happened. Then summoning him, his lord said to him, 'You wicked slave, I forgave you all that debt because you pleaded with me. Should you not also have had mercy on your fellow slave, in the same way that I had mercy on you?' And his lord, moved with anger, handed him over to the torturers until he should repay all that was owed him. My heavenly Father will also do the same to you, if each of you does not forgive his brother from your heart."

Let's break down this story to truly understand what Jesus is trying to teach us. It begins with a question of how many times must we forgive a brother who has sinned against us. The key word there is "brother", i.e. close relationship who has sinned against us. Peter isn't asking how many times he would have to forgive someone he doesn't know. If we all look back on our lives, it is easier to forgive someone you don't know, than to forgive someone close to you who hurts you. The closer the person is, the harder forgiveness is. Jesus' response is a seemingly excessive number. And in our modern culture, we would never imagine being able to forgive someone that many times. We would call that a toxic relationship. But what is Jesus trying to get across? First, we must realize that forgiveness and trust are not the same thing. I can choose to forgive someone and still not trust them. Trust is the foundation we build a relationship on with the understanding that I am for you and you are for me. Forgiveness is releasing a person from any expectations to repay what they have done to you or change any of their behaviors. These two words are different and we must understand that. I am only addressing forgiveness not rebuilding trust. Jesus never said to trust such a person, but He has called us to forgive.

The story continues with a parable that Jesus relates to what the Kingdom of God is like. Anytime Jesus reveals something that is like the Kingdom of God, it is vital that we lean in and listen to learn the truth He is speaking. The Kingdom of God is the kingdom we belong to, the one we are called to release on the earth, and the one we will one

day live in for eternity with Him. We can break the parable down like this: The Kingdom is likened to a king who
has slaves who owe him money. As he begins to settle
the debts with his slaves, he immediately comes across
one who owes a debt he cannot pay. The king begins to
say you will lose everything and be thrown into prison and
still will not be able to pay back this debt. The debt was
10,000 talents. A talent was a monetary value worth about
15 years of labor.[2] If we do the math, he owed a debt that
would take him 150,000 years to pay off. This slave throws
himself on the ground before the king to beg for mercy.
The king felt compassion and forgave the slave's debt.
This reminds me of a verse we already highlighted in Matthew 9:12-13, "...It is not those who are healthy who need
a physician, but those who are sick. But go and learn what
this means: 'I desire compassion, and not sacrifice,' for I
did not come to call the righteous, but sinners." The king
is revealing that mercy and forgiveness of unforgivable
debts is what his kingdom is like.

The story continues though with a turn of events. The
same slave who was just forgiven and was able to keep
his family from being sold goes out to one of his fellow
slaves who owes him. In anger he starts choking the slave
demanding repayment of 100 denarii. A denarius was a

day's wage for a laborer.[3] This slave owed him 100 days worth of money, compared to 150,000 years worth of money. The fellow slave throws himself on the ground and begs for mercy, but the slave who had been forgiven does not show mercy and instead has his fellow slave imprisoned until he could pay back what he owed him. Jesus ends the parable saying the king took the first slave and handed him over to the torturers until he could repay the debt and then says, "My heavenly Father will also do the same to you, if each of you does not forgive his brother from your heart" (Matthew 18:35).

The Debt of Sin

The story speaks of a greater reality. There is a debt of sin that humanity will never be able to repay. It was the debt of disobedience to God in the Garden of Eden and the debt that was only forgiven at the cross. Jesus models true forgiveness. Romans 6:23 says, "For the wages of sin is death, but the free gift of God is eternal life in Christ Jesus our Lord," and He is also our living hope. The cost of sin for a person is death. In the Garden of Eden, Adam and Eve created a debt of death when they obeyed the devil and sinned against God. This debt was so severe it is similar to the first slave in the parable. A debt that couldn't be solved in multiple lifetimes. Humanity continued to sin and continues to sin to the present day. Remember forgiveness isn't about a person changing, but a choice for the person who experienced the pain. This is why 1 John 4:19 is so profound, "We love, because He first loved us," and Ephesians 5:1-2, "Therefore be imitators of God, as beloved children; and walk in love, just as Christ also loved you and gave Himself up [for us], an offering and a sacrifice to God as a fragrant aroma." Forgiveness is never initiated by the offender. Humanity didn't initiate cleaning up our mess with God. God the Father and Jesus the Son initiated the plan of redemption and forgiveness to forgive humanity's debt. **The one who gave everything out of love chose to forgive the world in spite of ever expecting the world to change or love Him in return.** "For God so loved the world, that He gave His only begotten Son, that whoever believes in Him shall not perish, but have eternal life. For God did not send the Son into the world to judge the world, but that the world might be saved through Him" (John 3:16-17). We see it in the very end of Jesus' mission, while on the cross as He is about to take His last breath He says, "Father forgive them for they know not what they do" (Luke 23:24).

Jesus came to release the debt from humanity and to

forgive those who would come to him and humble themselves to receive mercy. If you have ever been given a substantial gift, you know how humbling it is to receive something you did not earn and could never repay. This is what Jesus has done for us. Psalms 103:1-4 says, "Bless the Lord, O my soul, and all that is within me, bless His holy name. Bless the Lord, O my soul, and forget none of His benefits; who pardons all your iniquities, who heals all your diseases; who redeems your life from the pit, who crowns you with loving kindness and compassion." This complete forgiveness and extravagant gift is supposed to crown the receiver with loving kindness and compassion. Why is that? Because it was compassion that led the king in the parable to forgive the debt, and a lack of compassion and love that led the slave to not forgive his fellow slave. Many of us can forget the debt of sin we have been forgiven of in this life. Jesus willingly laid down His life and gave us Himself to forgive our debt. The only thing He asks in return is our heart to love Him and follow Him. Many times we are the slave that has been forgiven of so much, yet find it hard to forgive the person who has hurt us. We can easily forget about the eternal realm of forgiveness over our souls and become a natural minded person who is willing to hold debts and offenses towards one another. We can become the Pharisees in the story from the last chapter who were ready to stone the woman caught in adultery instead of forgiving her. Too often we forget what He has done for us and the cost of our salvation, and that forgetfulness is revealed in how we choose to forgive one another.

How Does One Forgive From the Heart?

There are 5 steps that I have found to walk through the process of forgiving someone from the heart. Why is it highlighted that God is asking us to forgive from the heart? There is a verse in Matthew 12:33-37 where Jesus is speaking that has a similar tone to Luke 6:43-45.

> Either make the tree good and its fruit good, or make the tree bad and its fruit bad; for the tree is known by its fruit. You brood of vipers, how can you, being evil, speak what is good? For the mouth speaks out of that which fills the heart. The good man brings out of his good treasure what is good; and the evil man brings out of his evil treasure what is evil. But I tell you that every careless word that people speak, they shall give an accounting for it on the day of judgment. For by your words you will be justified, and by your words you will be condemned.

These verses chillingly reveal the reality that we can't fake forgiveness or merely go through the motions. We can liken our hearts to a garden, and we decide what grows in our hearts. The fruit of unforgiveness grows and ends up coming out of our mouth in the form of bitterness or resentment. Our job on this earth is to cultivate the spiritual garden of our heart and create a space that produces good fruit that can be seen and experienced by the people around us. Out of the overflow of our hearts we will reveal through our words the level of forgiveness and freedom we are walking in. As we begin to break down these five steps practically, remember that each one is simple, but like most things is easier said than done.

1. Face the Offense in a Safe Place

The first step to begin the process of forgiveness is to face the pain, offense, situation, struggle, or area of our lives or person that has caused us pain, disappointment, anger, fear, or any other emotions we need to forgive for. This is an important step as it begins the process. How can we forgive a debt we don't know the amount of? Too many people try to avoid pain and want to quickly have people forgive without the acknowledgment of the debt that has been created through the painful scenario. This process of facing the offense also allows someone to face the fear they have been running from, like the fear that they are to blame, that it isn't that big of a deal, or that it was only a little pain. If someone stole 1 million dollars from you, but someone told you to act as though it was only $1,000.00 there would be a big discrepancy in your ability to forgive them. There would also be a lack of validation a person needs from another individual to say how painful that experience would be.

Humans need validation to not feel crazy, but so many times in our forgiveness process we want to bypass validating that a situation was painful or unjust. In an effort to create powerful people, we bypass any form of someone feeling like a victim out of fear they will become one. Our lack of facing offense or pain, though, is setting people up to live a life constantly producing fruit in their hearts and lives that they don't want. Forgiveness restores the standard, but we have to know what standard was broken in order to restore it.

Take time in the presence of God and ask the Holy Spirit if there is any unresolved pain in your life that He is giving you the grace to overcome and forgive in this season. This is a hard step because many people will quickly say no to avoid ever looking at it. If you find you are having a hard time placing if someone has hurt you, there is another way to reveal what is happening in your heart. Get a journal and call it a pain journal. Only write painful things in here, to keep it separate from other journals you use for your life. The reason behind this is sometimes pain makes us feel deep, scary emotions and words about other people, that once we can get out we no longer feel. It is nice to have a place that is dedicated to these dumps from our hearts that we might not even fully believe, but we have to get off our chest.

How Do You Begin This Step?

- Begin by asking yourself if there is anyone you are annoyed or angry with right now? From there start to write what you are feeling down.
- Ask the Holy Spirit if there is unresolved pain in your life that He is providing the grace for you to face. Write down what you feel, see or experience.
- Find a leader or mentor who you trust, who is safe to hear painful things for them to help you walk in the light and into forgiveness.

2. Face the Impact of the Pain in Your Life

This is the part of the process that most people never step into when they are walking out the forgiveness process. Most people can face the painful event or offense, but what truly allows a person to forgive from the heart is when they are willing to face the impact or effects that the painful event or moment has had on their life. It is the process of getting honest to cleanse our souls. It moves us out of addressing just a painful moment, and into the impact that moment has had on our lives. For many of us we have forgiven the event of one of our parents walking out on our family, or the leader that controlled and manipulated us, or the friend that backstabbed us, but what most of us have never forgiven is the way that event has impacted our lives. Dad walking out at a young age is hard, but the pain was residual because Dad's choice had a lasting effect on our family and us personally. The friend that backstabbed us that led to an ongoing struggle to trust new friends. Mom being controlling out of her own fears has led to us constantly feeling a need for control and has ruined multiple relationships. We can't just forgive Mom for when she was controlling, or Dad for the day he walked out, or the friend for the backstabbing moment. We must forgive them for the impact that moment has caused in our lives. This is where the scary deep emotions reside, it's not in the past memory, but the present effects of the pain in our lives. The gardens of our hearts can too often be filled with pollutants from these painful emotional effects that we never let out and resolve.

How Do You Begin This Step?

- In your pain journal begin the process of picking a person or event that has caused significant pain and take time to journal how you feel about this person or event. Get specific with how you were or are impacted.

- This is a moment of complete vulnerability. Many times people try to protect people we love that have hurt us, and in doing so we never reach that level of honesty to truly express the pain they have caused. Be as real as possible.

- Once you have journaled those things, you now know what you are truly trying to forgive.

3. Forgive

Now that you have faced the pain and the impact of the event on your life, and how these things have actually made you feel, you can begin the process of forgiveness. Why is now the time? Because you have an understanding of the debt that is owed to you from the other person, and what you are actually forgiving. Many people say I forgive you without knowing what they are truly forgiving. This process is going through each painful moment or impact on your life and outloud saying you forgive the person for it. I know it can sound redundant, until you do it. It is liberating to address each area that has haunted us or caused us pain and to hear ourselves forgive them. If we break it down, we could forgive someone of $1,000 debt by one swift action, or we can forgive each of the purchases that built up the $1,000 debt. Both are forgiven, but one has an understanding of exactly what they are forgiving. For those painful events from people, we want to fully express what happened, so that future moments won't trigger unresolved pain from our past. The heart of forgiveness is to restore the standard and love in a relationship. It doesn't mean we have rebuilt trust with a person, just that we have restored the standard and love.

How Do You Begin This Step?

- Outloud forgive the person for each painful event or impact that the event has had on your life.
- Event example, "Dad I forgive you for leaving our family when I was 10." This is an example of forgiving an event.
- Impact example, "Dad I forgive you for making me feel that I wasn't enough for you to stay."

4. Release them from any expectations

This is an important step that many want to avoid. In the same way that Jesus released our debt before we changed, "while we were still sinners Christ died for us" (Romans 5:8), He is asking us to release people of their debt regardless if they ever change. In these moments we are becoming more like Jesus as we step into releasing debt for people who aren't going to change, and probably don't deserve this. **It is the mercy of God being revealed through us.** Mercy means not getting the punishment we deserve because of our sins. In the same way, we are releasing people from punishment or debt even when they don't deserve it. This is hard for people with strong justice meters who feel people need to change before they can be forgiven. If you fall into this category, it's okay, I do as well. How I have overcome my own justice meter is to remember the justice of the cross. "He made Him who knew no sin to be sin on our behalf, so that we might become the righteousness of God in Him" (2 Corinthians 5:21). Jesus took on our sin and forgave our sin when He had no sin. He is the example of true justice where on our worst day we are still forgivable. In this same way on someone else's worst day, they are still forgivable.

If we fail to release people from the expectations to

change or apologize, we can find ourselves trapped in a brain loop. That moment we keep repeating a painful event where there is no resolve because the person is gone, passed away, or won't repent. These loops of repeat look similar in our brain to trauma. Trauma is an unresolvable event that we repeat over and over in our minds as we can't find a way to fix it. Without a solution, we can get stuck in a painful traumatic moment for years. How do we break this repetitive brain cycle? We find a higher road of justice and forgiveness that doesn't require the person or event to change but instead releases the person or situation from any expectations to change. It's finally releasing your parent who walked out on your family from ever coming back. It's releasing the friend who gossiped about you from ever changing. It is coming to grips that true forgiveness doesn't require the other person to change.

How Do You Begin This Step?

- We need to take a moment to have a revelation of how Jesus views justice. He gives mercy even when we don't deserve it. Meditate on the story of the women in Luke 7:36-50 from the last chapter. Think about how much you have been forgiven of. In light of this revelation, it opens us up to be able to love people and forgive them from our hearts.

- Take a moment and write down every expectation you have of the person who hurt you, and how you want them to change.
- Outloud release them from each expectation you wrote down.

5. The Process of Loving Well

The final step is taking a moment to gain God's heart and affection for the person. He loves them and has thoughts about them. As we step into His heart for them, we can finish the forgiveness process by praying a prayer of blessing over them. This is challenging, but also revealing of where we are at in the debt forgiveness process. As we forgive more debt and release the person, the easier it becomes to pray for them and gain God's heart for them. This is where justice and mercy are experienced on the Earth. This is also how we continue to walk out the greatest commandment. "Love the Lord your God with all your heart, and with all your soul and with all your mind, this is the great and foremost commandment." The second is like it, "you shall love your neighbor as yourself" (Matt 22:37-38).

How Do You Begin This Step?

- Ask the Holy Spirit to reveal God's heart for the person or situation that was painful. Write down what you hear.

- Ask the Holy Spirit where He was during the situation that was painful. Write down what you hear.

- Take a moment to pray for the person who hurt you.

Personal Story of Walking Through the 5 Steps

As we walk through the steps of forgiveness I will share a personal story of how I have used this 5 step process to find forgiveness towards people that I imagined I could never forgive. There was a leader for a short season in my life who had a great impact on my life positively and negatively. My ability to sort through the God stuff and forgive the human painful stuff has set me up to become the person I am today. My first step was to face the painful scenarios of that season. To give a brief version, there was a leader in my life who I fully trusted, who struggled with tendencies of control, manipulation, and creating this constant feeling that they were always right and I was always wrong. Every encounter, interaction, or revelation from God I thought I received was met with a diminishing of who I was, or what I walked in, and an overemphasis on my need for their leadership in my life. I never felt I could make this leader proud or had what it took to be seen. Mixed into this scenario were legalistic rules, harsh feedback through punishment, disempowerment, bad theology, and a constant sense that he held a higher revelation of God and His kingdom than anyone else in the church or my life. There was constant communication of how my parents could no longer help me in my walk with God, or the senior leader of the church because this leader over me knew more about God's Kingdom and His ways than anyone else. This was the start of four painful years of my life that left me feeling more insecure, powerless, afraid, anxious, and confused about leadership and God than ever before. I was scared that if this was the model of leadership, I didn't want leadership in my life. This season and the harsh words spoken to me created a deep pain and offense in my heart and isolation from other leaders in the church. A few years after moving away from this painful leader I took my first step by finally opening up to a friend about the season as honestly as I could face it at that moment. I was on a houseboat, and this man on our team was asking me questions about my life, and out of nowhere, I started to share about my season. As I shared just the facts of what had happened he responded by saying, "Rory I think you were under a cult-like leader." I didn't know what to do with that so I stared at him as I felt deep emotion starting to come up in the form of tears. The tears felt so sudden I was afraid of them and did everything I could to push them down. I knew this was a significant moment and that I had unresolved pain I had not dealt with. After this moment I took time and journaled and found a leader I trusted who I shared everything with. I began the process of forgiveness. With this leader, I verbally faced all the pain and disappointment and harsh words that were spoken over me by this man. I went through and intentionally felt the pain and forgave him. Then I took time to release him outloud of any expectation to ever be able to clean up the pain he had caused me. The debt was big and the impact this pain had on my life was evident. It took me more than one moment to fully forgive this man. After a few months of continuing to open up when painful things came up, forgive, and release, I finally found myself able to pray for him and experience God's heart for him. It was at this moment I knew I had truly forgiven him. I had experienced the supernatural power of God to forgive someone I felt I could never forgive.

Our Choice Still Matters

What happens if we know we are supposed to forgive and choose not to? James 4:17 says, "Therefore, to one who knows the right thing to do and does not do it, to him it is sin." The ending of the parable in Matthew 18 reveals this scenario playing out. It was assumed by the king that the slave would forgive his fellow slave of the small debt since he himself was forgiven of so much. But as we saw that didn't happen and the parable ends with the slave who had originally been forgiven by the king being handed over to torturers or the demonic realm because of his unforgiveness and Jesus says that the Father will do the same to those who don't forgive. There is also another verse that backs up the ending of the parable of the two slaves. Matthew 6:9-14 teaches us how to pray, but it also reveals a strong connection of forgiveness found in the place of prayer, and the effects of choosing not to forgive.

> Pray, then, in this way: "Our Father who is in heaven, hallowed be your name. Your kingdom come. Your will be done, on earth as it is in heaven. Give us this day our daily bread. And forgive us our debts, as we also have forgiven our debtors. And do not lead us into temptation, but deliver us from evil. [For Yours is the kingdom and the power and the glory forever. Amen.]" For if you forgive others for their transgressions, your heavenly Father will also forgive you. But if you do not forgive others, then your Father will not forgive your transgressions.

The word transgressions means, "a lapse or deviation from truth or uprightness; sin, or misdeed."[4] Our own forgiveness from the Father is held in tension with whether we choose to forgive one another. Our decision to hold onto unforgiveness creates a doorway for the demonic to enter our lives.

Accusation

The doorway unforgiveness opens can have different effects, one of which is accusation. A spirit of accusation holds someone's sins against them. It is the demonic voice that reminds an individual of past mistakes, past sins, and creates a deceptive reality of the person's identity that feels real. The reason the spirit of accusation feels so real and powerful, is because it has authority in a believer's life who has chosen not to face pain and forgive. Revelation 12:10 says, "Now the salvation, and the power, and the kingdom of our God and the authority of His Christ have come, for the accuser of our brethren has been thrown down, he who accuses them before our God day and night. And they overcame him because of the blood of the Lamb and because of the word of their testimony, and they did not love their life even when faced with death." The blood of the Lamb forgives us and helps us overcome the accuser of the church. When we don't forgive, the Father no longer forgives us through Jesus' blood which lets the accuser have access to our lives again. This can seem scary, or we can gain an understanding of who God is through these verses and the fear of God in order to walk in His ways and choose to forgive. People are often looking for the perks of salvation without the cost and sacrifice of walking in the way Jesus walked.

Forgiveness is one of the most powerful things a believer can do to reveal Jesus to the world. It is also a safeguard against the demonic realm having access and influence in our lives. Even though it can be scary, painful, or sometimes feel impossible, God has given every person the ability to forgive in the same way we have been forgiven. Before we continue with this book I want to speak encouragement and strength over you. As we take the risk to face our pain, forgive, and restore our view of God, we ultimately get to return to the proper view of ourselves. Pain distorts reality while forgiveness clears the lens for us to see properly. This includes seeing God properly, our past properly, or present, and our future through the eyes of hope. The next chapters of this book focus on how facing these hard things change our lives and creates the space for belonging in His glory to become our reality.

The road of belonging is hard, but the cost of not walking on it is even harder. The next parts of this book focus on new beliefs, mindsets, and tools to walk in an atmosphere of belonging in the glory and Presence of God and returning to the original intent of humanity: to walk with God fully seen, fully known, and confident that we are loved.

The Path Forward

1. Take time to review the "How Do You Begin This Step?" section of each of the five forgiveness steps. Find a mentor to bring into this process with you as you start to forgive the different people in your life.

2. Sometimes we can feel overwhelmed by the amount of people we need to forgive. My goal was to start with one and walk through that before tackling the next one. As we focus on one person we find ourselves gaining momentum and breakthrough that helps us as we tackle the different painful things in our lives.

Chapter 7:
The Most
Important
Questions

On this journey through life, I want to assure you that you are not crazy, there is nothing wrong with you, and you are about to discover all the incredible things that are right with you–the things that make you, you. But the only way to truly discover yourself is to truly discover who God is and how He made you. He created you, knows you, loves you, and made you in His image. Psalm 100:3, "Know that the LORD Himself is God; It is He who has made us, and not we ourselves." He is the only one who can tell you who you are. Culture can't tell you who you are, social media can't, and famous people of our day can't because none of those people created you. God created you and therefore is the only one who is intimately aware of who He created you to be. To know ourselves more we have to get to know Him. As we discussed previously, painful moments create skewed perspectives, including a skewed perspective of God the Father and His nature which, in turn gives us a skewed view of ourselves. Now that we have begun the process of facing our pain and clearing our lens to see God clearly, we can begin to discover who we are and His desire for our lives.

How dangerous is a wrong view of ourselves? There was a young boy once who was twelve years old. He had a variety of painful moments that affected the lens he saw himself through. The first subtle moment was when he joined a new athletic team and after six weeks of being on the team, one of the boys had a birthday party. The teammate having the party walked up to this young boy and said, "Hey, I didn't invite you because I don't know you very well." All the other teammates and coach left practice early to go to this party, leaving behind this young man and one other teammate who was an outcast in the group. That day was his first recollection of feeling like a loser. It was a small snowball that eventually picked up speed.

The young man started struggling in social settings. Quietness and anxiety became his friends. He sought to fit in at all cost. He switched teams and the new coach was even worse than the old one. "Fat, you are so fat," the new coach would constantly tell this young man. This went on for four years. During this time the young man tried a youth group. Even though the group was small, social anxiety had taken its toll. He did his best to be "invisible" in the room of people. The snowball effect of the wrong view of himself was gaining momentum and size in this young man's life. It was driving a stronger force of self-hatred within him.

This self-hatred began an insatiable desire for acceptance at any cost and heavy feelings of sadness when it was not met. The instability in the young man's life was making him a slave to the need for acceptance. It led him to struggle with his weight, happiness, and fear of man. He needed people to approve of him and was easily deceived by people. This led to many relationships where he was controlled, manipulated, the butt of every joke, and the tag along instead of the friend. The lens of self-hatred was fully set, and by the end of high school he was no longer able to discern or feel what was good or bad. All he saw through was the lens of please accept me or I'm rejected.

Because of this lens, he began rejecting people before they ever rejected him because it hurt less. Isolation, loneliness, and fear were his friends. This young man was me. Our need for acceptance, if not fulfilled with true belonging in His glorious Presence, makes us susceptible to codependent and controlling relationships, and ultimately deception. When a person fears that they don't belong they will do whatever it takes to find acceptance in order to stabilize themselves in life. Why is that? Belonging creates a confidence inside of a human that stabilizes them. It is a power so strong, yet so underemphasized in culture. It was the driving force that led me to go from my mean, intense, constantly critical coach that I never felt enough under, to serve a man right out of high school that was full of control and manipulation that I later realized left me more broken and wounded than before I met him. Whenever someone is looking for acceptance they will bypass wisdom and place themselves in unhealthy relationships where their pain goes from bad to worse.

I have seen this many times over the years with different young people. The scenario can play out with relationships. A guy sees a girl and is interested. The girl is not sure she is interested but likes the attention. The guy quickly says things like, "You are beautiful. I love you. I've never felt this way." These words feel like water in the desert of the girl's soul. After all, she can barely look at herself in the mirror and be happy with what she sees. She is grateful she started that diet when she did. She is fixated on the guy's words. He is grateful that a girl who feels out of his league is responding to him. They both are finding acceptance in each other's words and it quickly turns physical. Neither of them want to stop the other because they both feel like this is the place of acceptance they have been longing for. What they don't know and they find out later is that false acceptance has an expiration date. The feelings fade, the fear sets back in, the anxiety of codependency and manipulation to keep each other in the relationship heightens, and eventually there is an ugly breakup, or worse a failed marriage. A lot of people think that only girls struggle with self-hatred and guys are just horny. There is a common misconception that it is only guys that take advantage of insecure girls. I hope to shine light on this and create a greater sense of awareness of the deep levels of self-hatred that are prevalent in our society with men and women.

Self-hatred is not about shrinking a waist size, whether you can grow facial hair, have the right personality, if you have the six pack, or any other external factor about yourself. Many people think that self-hatred can be solved by changing the external thing a person hates about themselves. This is why we see anti-aging creams showing up in peoples' thirties, botox and plastic surgery, and health fads popping up, and ads trying to show us something we should hate about ourselves and how buying a product will help us not hate that anymore, as if an external change could impact an internal reality. Self-hatred is an internal belief system that cannot be solved by external changes. The person who feels fat can lose the weight and will still struggle to believe they are pretty or good looking enough. You see it when girls that are tiny are still dieting or guys that have six packs but still feel they aren't strong enough. When the lenses of our minds hold up an unrealistic image of ourselves that we must obtain, we have to change the lens internally.

How do we change an internal lens? We must look at the lens like a structure full of clear bricks. Each brick needs to be dismantled and a new lens needs to be built in our minds. Another way to say this is "tearing down strongholds of thinking and replacing them with strongholds of Truth". We already reviewed this idea of tearing down thoughts that exalt themselves above the nature of God. In the same way a thought can come against God's nature, a thought or stronghold can also come against God's design of us. As we partner with self-hatred we are also partnering with the idea that God made a mistake while creating us or that He is a poor designer. Now, we would never say these words out loud, but that is why I am writing them in this book: so we can read them, recognize they are lies, and agree to let the truth sink in. Any place where we have a stronghold of lies is the place we will be deceived. For example, when someone has a stronghold of self-hatred in their lives it is easy to be deceived by their emotions, feelings, and desires. Those things not submitted to Truth become a raging fire that is never quenched, which continually needs more to satisfy the hole within the person's life. Emotions, feelings, and desires promise many things but never come through. Why? Because emotions, feelings, and desires are good servants and terrible masters. If we have a stronghold of self-hatred in our lives, things that are good become a snare to us and drive us into things and places we never wanted to go to.

So how do we tear down a stronghold? I think of this process as a three part system: Repent, Replace, and Rebuild. Each part is an intentional tool used in the process.

Repent

If you are thinking about running to an altar and weeping as you read this word, my hope is to expand our minds and understanding of the word repentance. We first need to understand that the word sin means to miss the mark or not walk in the standards and values of heaven. Repent is a word that means "to change one's mind."[1] It is a word to describe seeing a place in our lives where we have sinned or missed the mark of God's Kingdom and we, in action, change the course of our lives to become synced again with His Kingdom. Repentance can be running to an altar and weeping, and it can also be daily taking thoughts captive about ourselves that aren't in God's mind about us and getting rid of them, and replacing them with the thoughts God does have about us.

As you start this process of repentance, you may be asking, "How do I recognize the thoughts that I need to repent of?" It can be hard to see destructive ways of thinking when they have become so familiar to our conscious mind. This is where some people start to find areas of wrong thinking, but can quickly dive too deeply internally to try and fix all the bad thinking and tear down all the bad strongholds. This isn't the goal, nor do I recommend this being the approach. If the goal of repentance is to tear down areas of lies in our lives and to replace them with truth, we have to know how we find truth. And who convicts us. Is it our conscience? In the Bible there are two key verses that reveal there is one person who convicts and reveals truth to us. Convenient that God would place both of these things in the same person.

In John 16:7-8 Jesus says, "But I tell you the truth, it is to your advantage that I go away; for if I do not go away, the Helper will not come to you; but if I go, I will send Him to you. And He, when He comes, will convict the world concerning sin and righteousness and judgment." The Holy Spirit was sent to earth to convict the world of sin. He is also called the Spirit of Truth. Just a few verses later in John 16:13 it says, "But when He, the Spirit of truth, comes, He will guide you into all the truth; for He will not speak on His own initiative, but whatever He hears, He will speak; and He will disclose to you what is to come." The Father has set up an incredible ability for us to step out of the strongholds of self-hatred and rejection by giving us His Holy Spirit. The One who convicts us of areas in our lives where we are missing His perfect will of the Kingdom is also the One who reveals divine truth. It is incredible that it is a relationship with the Holy Spirit that gives way for us to repent. Our job was never to self-diagnose problems, or to do a deep dive to fix us, it was to yield to the Holy Spirit and respond as He brings things to light. He will never reveal a place in our lives that we need to repent of without releasing the grace and truth to walk it out in freedom and to build the new lens of truth.

Replace

The second thing to building a stronghold of truth in our minds is to replace the lies out loud that we have just repented of with the truth. This sounds interesting and to some a little over the top, but our minds are truly wonderful things that God has created. One of the most fascinating things about our minds though, is something called plasticity. It is the ability for our mind to constantly change and create new pathways of thinking. It means our minds are not concrete, they are moldable. What is even more fascinating is that the human mind does not lose any level of its plasticity the older a person gets. This means that at any age we can change the way we think.[2] It is also important to know that the area of our minds that read information and hear information are different. This means internally repenting and then externally renouncing lies is necessary for the two different areas of our brain to reset with the new pathway of truth we are creating. The more we out loud renounce lies and replace them with the truth, our brains start to recognize that the lie we are saying is not what we want to be focused on. The more we declare truth out loud, the more our brains pick it up as a repetitive thought that gets stored into our thinking. This process is pivotal and is the step that most people do once, and then forget about the next time the thought comes around. Remember, ways of thinking are not changed overnight. Repentance is instant, replacing lies is a process. This leads to the last step–rebuilding.

Rebuild

This is the final process of creating new strongholds and new ways of thinking. There are a few different tools we can use to rebuild new strongholds of truth in our lives.

1. The Word

The first is the Word of God aka the Bible. The Bible is not just a book with words, pages, chapters, and authors. It is the key to accessing and walking in the life God has called us to. Hebrews 4:12 says, "For the word of God is living and active and sharper than any two-edged sword, and piercing as far as the division of soul and spirit, of both joints and marrow, and able to judge the thoughts and intentions of the heart." The Bible was never meant to be read once and retained as information. It is a book that is filled with the life of God and carries the power within its words to transform your life, activate His promises, and release His Kingdom into your situation.

As we begin to understand the power of the Word and how it is living and active, we begin to understand that it can be used to renew our minds. God didn't call us to think differently without telling us what that should look like. He also promises in Isaiah 55:9-11,

> For as the heavens are higher than the earth, So are my ways higher than your ways and my thoughts than your thoughts. For as the rain and the snow come down from heaven, and do not return there without watering the earth, and making it bear and sprout and furnishing see to the sower and bread to the eater; so will My word be which goes forth from My mouth; it will not return to Me empty, without accomplishing what I desire, and without succeeding in the matter for which I sent it.

God created His word to carry power and, when declared,

His word accomplishes what it was sent to do. When rebuilding strongholds of truth in our minds, declaration is necessary to activate God's Word and send it to build in our minds what it has been sent to do.

2. Thanksgiving

Enter His gates with thanksgiving, and His courts with praise. Give thanks to Him, bless His name. Psalm 100:4 illustrates the pathway to more of Jesus and it starts with thanksgiving. The process of building strongholds of truth has to be a forward momentum into the Presence of Jesus. That momentum has always started with thanksgiving. We come to a person's house and have to knock, ring the doorbell, and then say hello as we enter. Coming into the Presence of God is similar. It starts with thanksgiving. This psalm is revealing the process of the Old Testament tabernacle, where the manifest Presence of God dwelt with man after the garden of Eden. The psalmist is illustrating that the way to enter the Presence of God is through thanksgiving. Not only does thankfulness give us access to God, it also dramatically impacts our mental health. Harvard Education wrote an article on the effects of gratitude on a person's life. In the article they wrote, "In positive psychology research, gratitude is strongly and consistently associated with greater happiness. Gratitude helps people feel more positive emotions, relish good experiences, improve their health, deal with adversity, and build strong relationships."[3]

Thankfulness is the process of thanking God out loud for what He has done in our lives. It is the intentional act of remembering all the testimonies, breakthroughs, and moments where God has come through, revealed Himself, and delivered us. As we begin to remember and thank God for what He has done, we create pathways of remembrance in our minds to lean on in times of struggle. God doesn't need our thankfulness. The act of remembering and being thankful sets us up to follow God and overcome seasons where our situation or circumstance doesn't match the God we know. In these seasons, remembering God's acts and ways in our lives sets us up to encounter Him. It is also a safeguard in our walks with God to continue to follow Him in hard seasons.

Thankfulness also creates an increase in our lives. Whatever we are thankful for, we set ourselves up like a magnet in the spiritual realm to attract more of it in our lives. If we are thankful for who God made us to be, we attract confidence in our identity. If we are thankful for the season we

are in, we attract favor and promotion. God is always looking for people who have discovered the power of thankfulness to increase the good things in their lives. Thanking God for His nature creates a bullseye on our lives to
encounter that aspect of His nature. Many times when we
are struggling we want to complain about our situations
thinking that will help us overcome them. In reality, being
thankful for God's nature sets us up to experience it more.

3. Praise

Praise is the second part of the verse in Psalm 100 and
is the action of declaring the nature of God. Thanksgiving and praise are connected, because as we remember
moments where God has come through. Those testimonies reveal God's nature. Praise is our ability to declare
the nature of God that has just been revealed to us. Many
people think praise is the fast song at the start of a church
service. This is not the case. Praise is our ability to declare
out loud the nature of God that we have discovered in
our lives. Here is an example of finding thanksgiving and
praise even in the midst of a painful situation that led to
breakthrough and intimacy with God.

Shofars Make Good Weapons Too

I was 21 years old and had just taken the leap of faith to move to a different city based on a word I felt I heard from God. I created this fantasy experience that was going to be waiting for me on the other side of this move because of my obedience to this word. I imagined a great job, amazing living space, and instant community. Have you ever imagined how a word was going to play out? To my surprise it went the exact opposite. The job I thought I was going to have fell through two days before I moved, I couldn't find an affordable place to live, and meeting new people was not my strong suit. After several weeks I finally scored a minimum wage job at an office supplies store, and after a few more weeks I found an affordable place to live where I had my own bedroom and shared bathroom. A couple months into the move and I was finally feeling some sort of stability. That is when "things" started to happen.

At first it was my leftovers going missing from the fridge, then all food was going missing in the house, then there were random people stopping by that looked less than reputable. Finally the event happened. It was just after 11pm on a Friday night and I had worked a closing shift. The woman who owned the house I rented from with her son had told me they were both going to be out of town for the weekend. Relieved was an understatement. I was excited to have the house to myself and be able to keep leftovers in the fridge for a few days. As I got to my house though, something wasn't right. In the yard were 10-15 people in a circle exchanging items for money as big puffs of smoke were rising above them. My brain was tired and instead of leaving, I pulled into the driveway and just stared at the scene. I realized they were looking at me and felt nervous to back away. Instead I thought if I can just get to my room I'll be okay.

Walking slowly to the door I passed the group, as I opened the screen door something else was waiting for me. The door to our house was open and inside was a group of people that smelled awful with a massive rag-gedy dog that I am convinced had a coat full of bugs. As I was trying to take the scene in, a man in a large black trenchcoat flew at me yelling, "Did you take my weed? Tell me, did you take my weed?" Confused, I finally got the words out and said, "No I didn't take your weed." I quickly shot down the hallway toward my room. As I shut the door behind me I remembered the door didn't have a lock. It dawned on me that I should have left. I quickly surveyed to see if there was anything that I could use as a weapon.

It's when I remembered my shofar. Just as I grabbed it there was a knock on the door of my room. I was ready to unleash it on whoever was going to walk through the door. I said, "Yes?" and to my relief my roommate responded, "I found my weed in my pocket."

My body exhaled but the pain of this season caught up to me. The whirlwind of doubt and pain flooded my mind as thoughts started to form against God. "Why did you bring me here? Why aren't you providing for me? Do you even see me?" The thoughts swirled as anxiety started to tighten my chest. I was feeling a mix of hopelessness, defeat, and anger. Did I miss God or is He just good to other people and not me? As I was about to take the bait of pain and disappointment to guide my lens of God, another thought hit me. I heard the voice of a woman named Leslie who had mentored me for a few years at this point. Her voice rang in my head as a faint calling in the midst of the other thoughts and it was a phrase she had said to me often: "God is Faithful." The phrase continued to ring through my mind and gained volume as I began to focus on it. It didn't make sense. Everything in my world wasn't working. How could God be faithful?

I then had another thought, if I am to break this swirl that I encounter every time I am in pain or disappointed I need to do something different in the middle of it. That night was the night. What better opportunity than a scenario that is less than ideal with no chance of it changing? Standing on my mattress I started to shout as loud as I could the song, "I sing because you are good!" Over and over I started to sing it and as I declared it I began to feel something show up in my room that I hadn't felt in a scenario like this. It was His Presence full of joy. So much joy. I started dancing around the room shouting the song as loud as I could until I was laughing full of the tangible Presence of Jesus. I then drifted to sleep.

Many of us want our scenarios to change before we praise or give thanks. We want God to prove Himself before we believe. God is waiting for our ability to praise and thank Him in the midst of hard and painful scenarios. That night taught me the power of remembering who God is and praising Him in the midst of any situation. What also transpired shortly after this moment was an increase of pay and hours at my job, a new living place that I could afford, and a new confidence in who God is regardless of what I am experiencing. It is time to activate our faith in hard moments of life to remember who God is and what He has done regardless of our current experience.

4. Hearing God's Voice

We gain the incredible ability to walk in a renewed mind through the Holy Spirit who reveals the Father's voice and thoughts to us. In 1 Corinthians 2:9-12 Paul writes,

> "Things which eye has not seen, and ear has not heard, and which have not entered the heart of man, all that God has prepared for those who love him." For to us God revealed them through the Spirit; for the Spirit searches all things, even the depths of God. For who among men knows the thoughts of a man except the spirit of the man which is in him? Even so the thoughts of God no one knows except the Spirit of God. Now we have received, not the spirit of the world, but the Spirit who is from God, so that we may know the things freely given to us by God.

Our ability to understand and hear God's voice to know what has been given to us comes from the Holy Spirit. Without the Holy Spirit, we aren't able to hear God's voice. Holy Spirit is the one who comes and reveals what the Father is saying, who Jesus is, and the things God has freely given to us who believe. In the process of rebuilding strongholds of truth, the Holy Spirit is key in revealing the voice of God that renews our minds. Paul ends 1 Corinthians 2:16 with a profound statement on the impact a relationship with the Holy Spirit will have on a believer's life. "For who has known the mind of the Lord that he will instruct Him? But we have the mind of Christ." This reality is the promise, and the destiny of every believer. To fully walk in the mind of Christ, a mind full of unwavering truth rooted in faith.

Two Most Important Questions to Answer

As we continue in this journey there are two questions that I had to settle in my heart for me to succeed in the longevity of overcoming pain, bad beliefs, and wrong views of myself and God. These two questions were, "God, what were you thinking when you created me?" And, "God how much do you love me?" These questions sound simple enough however many believers are not confident in the answers. I've heard people try to pull on spiritual jargon to try to religiously answer these questions, but the soul who discovers through revelation the answers becomes the person who can find true belonging. These questions provoke the deep need to discover the God of eternity and what He thinks of us. His thoughts are the ones we need to define us. If we are undefined by the thoughts of

God about us, we will find inaccurate definitions about us from the world around us. The answers create intimacy in our walks with God and become anchors of truth for us to declare over ourselves as we are on this journey of renewing our minds. It is Paul's plea, "And do not be conformed to this world, but be transformed by the renewing of your mind, so that you may prove what the will of God is, that which is good and acceptable and perfect" (Romans 12:2). If we renew our minds in God we discover His will that is good for our lives. If we don't, we conform to the world around us and what the world thinks and expects of us. God is looking for a people who will discover who He is through an intimate relationship. His desire is to draw people into His glorious Presence in order to reveal Himself and His nature. It is time we discover the God who is "compassionate and gracious, slow to anger and abounding in loving kindness" (Psalm 103:8).

As you begin this process of renewing your mind and replacing strongholds of lies with strongholds of truth you will discover how to recognize what is your pain and what pain you are picking up from someone else. It is important to recognize what walls you are tearing down and rebuilding. This whole process though is not to become a better person, or to become a healthier person. The goal is to find God your Father, Creator, and Designer of who you are, and to discover His thoughts, love, delight, and joy over you. Transformation is the outcome of a renewed mind of truth. It is not enough to play mental gymnastics to try and think differently. Our job is to find the God who "makes known to [us] the path of life; In [whose] presence is fullness of joy; in [whose] right hand there is pleasures forever" (Psalm 16:11). He is the God that has given us "Everything for life and godliness" (2 Peter 1:3). As we find God our Father through His Son Jesus we discover who we are truly created to be. In His glory is the clearest revelation of life, hope, joy, calling, future, blessing, favor, family, marriage, finance, culture, everything is found clear in the glory of God as we discover the place of belonging in Him.

Meditation Questions

1. Ask God, "How much do you love me?"
2. Ask God, "What were you thinking when you created me?"
3. Ask God, "What strongholds of truth have I built in my life?"
4. What lies have been revealed through the Holy Spirit as I have read this book that I am ready to Repent, Replace, and Rebuild in my thinking?

The Path Forward

1. How do we find this truth? There is only one truth that we can use to build healthy strongholds in our lives, and that is the word of God. Here are some foundational verses to meditate on to create a new stronghold of truth. Take time to write down what God is speaking to you about from each verse.

   - Jeremiah 29:11
   - 1 John 3:1
   - Psalm 103:1-5
   - Isaiah 61:1-3
   - 2 Corinthians 5:17-21
   - John 3:16-17

Chapter 8:
True Hope Does
Not Disappoint

It was the first hot day of the Redding summer hitting
a high of 108 degrees. I was hanging out with a young
man who I have had the privilege of walking with for the
last several years. We drank our smoothies in our usual
spot, shared our weekly updates about school and life,
but this time he shared a testimony of a breakthrough he
had that caught my attention. He shared how impactful a
moment at church was a few days before where I had led
a transition moment and went after placing our hope in
an outcome instead of in the nature of Jesus. As he was
in the room he realized that there was a place he had put

his hope that wasn't in God but in an outcome. When this young man had first moved to Redding with his family, he lived in a beautiful home in Palo Cedro. A few years later a painful event happened in his family that forced them to move from this home he loved, and the last place where his family was all together. In this moment at church, the Holy Spirit revealed to him that he had placed an expectation and a hope that one day God was going to give their family that house back. He had dreamed of it for years, praying and believing, until this Sunday when he realized he had placed his hope in getting back into this house as if it was God's promise for his life and family. He was convinced that God was going to restore the house. That Sunday he had an epiphone moment where he realized God never promised that but that God promised He would be with him. The young man made a comment to me that will forever stick with me. He said, "God's promise isn't to get our family back into that house. I now realize that is never going to happen. God's promise is that He is our promised land. He is my promised land." This young man had received a revelation that few find. God is the promise, He is who we put our hope in, and He is the one who can make all things new and restore all things. He is sufficient regardless of an outcome.

Disappointment and the God of All Hope

"Hope deferred makes the heart sick, but desire fulfilled is a tree of life" (Proverbs 13:12). Hope is the eager anticipation that good is just around the corner. Hope is the substance scientists have found that is formed again in a person who chooses to forgive.[1] Hope is a powerful substance that has a profound impact on our lives. As we discover areas we are rebuilding strongholds of truth, we have to face areas where we have placed our hope in an outcome or promise that God never said. Hoping in something can be done in vain. People call wishful thinking "hope" as if they are one and the same. That can't be farther from the truth. Hope is only found through a person.

> Blessed be the God and Father of our Lord Jesus Christ, who according to His great mercy has caused us to be born again to a living hope through the resurrection of Jesus Christ from the dead, to obtain an inheritance which is imperishable and undefiled and will not fade away, reserved in heaven for you, who are protected by the power of God through faith for a salvation ready to be revealed in the last time. (1 Peter 1:3-5)

We are born again into a living hope for the salvation and

union of being eternally with Christ. Our hope is rooted in the reality of being born again, and the finished work of the cross, which sets us up to believe that good is always on its way. "Goodness and lovingkindness will follow me all the days of my life, and I will dwell in the house of the Lord forever" (Psalm 23:6). Hope in his goodness regardless of what it looks like. Only in Jesus is there a "hope that does not disappoint" (Romans 5:5).

Hope is not an expectation of something specific happening. Hope is an expectation and confidence in the person of Jesus being who He says He is in our lives and anticipating Him to show up. This anticipation is in good things coming, but we don't always know what it will look like. When our hope has a set desired outcome it is no longer hope but expectations. This is different than hope deferred. The word "deferred" has the connotation of something being dragged on or drawn out.[2] When it feels like we are in the valley and we can't see the other side, or we are waiting for goodness to surprise us, these are the moments where hope can feel shaky and in these places, if we aren't careful our hearts can become sick. This is an important place to understand belonging and who God is. If we aren't aware of what hope is and where we are placing our hope, we can become disillusioned and disappointed in God. "The God of all hope" (Romans 15:13). This is why Proverbs 4:23 commands us to "Watch over your heart with all diligence for from it flow the springs of life." Our hearts are our responsibility to watch over, and our hope in God is our responsibility to keep in the right place. Not a hope in an outcome, but a hope in a person and in the finished work of salvation that has already been provided for us.

Paul exhorts the church to "exult in our tribulations, knowing that tribulation brings about perseverance; and perseverance, proven character; and proven character, hope; and hope does not disappoint, because the love of God has been poured out within our hearts through the Holy Spirit who was given to us" (Romans 5:3-5). God has revealed the path of finding hope that doesn't disappoint when it is placed in God, His nature, and the understanding of the cross of Christ. He displayed walking through painful situations and scenarios in obedience to discover hope including the hope of the Father resurrecting Him, the hope of a church who would become His bride, and the hope of a glorious future together with us again. Christ pushed through the pain because of the hope of the good thing that was coming. Humanity reconnected to the Father and restored in all its brilliance. Paul continues to reveal the power of this hope we have because of Jesus and the impact it has on the church and our place of belonging and confidence in God.

> Now I rejoice in my sufferings for your sake, and in my flesh I do my share on behalf of His body, which is the church, in filling up what is lacking in Christ's afflictions. Of this church I was made a minister according to the stewardship from God bestowed on me for your benefit, so that I might fully carry out the preaching of the word of God, that is the mystery which has been hidden from the past ages and generations, but has now been manifested to His saints, to whom God willed to make know what is the riches of the glory of this mystery among the Gentiles, which is Christ in you, the hope of Glory. (Colossians 1:24-27)

We can only understand the hope that doesn't disappoint, when it is placed in the finished work of Christ that opened the door to the glory of God. Hope in Christ is a hope that lasts. Hope in Christ is the hope of confidence and belonging. It is the hope in perfect union with God our Father because of the cross. The cross and Christ's suffering is the very place that hope broke forth into a believer's life and is the only place that hope is sustained in a believer's life.

It pains me to see how much disappointment has crept into believers who serve the God of all hope and who have been given a living hope. This disappointment creates a barrier between us and God, and hinders us from experiencing his glory and presence in the place of belonging to Him. The very part of His nature of hope and being the God that constantly has good things in store for us, can be the thing we get disillusioned and hurt by. When we try to control the outcome we end up losing every time. What do I mean by this? When our hope is actually an expectation instead of hope in God, it sets us up to create a pass-fail performance moment for God in our lives. If God does what we expect we joyfully serve Him and follow Him. If the outcome is different than what we expect or want, then we say God has let us down. This in turn leads us back to the orphan mindset that pulls us out of the place of confident belonging in God. But when our hope is in God and His nature regardless of what it looks like, our walk with Him becomes the grand adventure and mystery it is designed to be.

The Three Young Men and the Wicked King

There is a story in the Bible that illustrates the true meaning of hope in God and how to trust in His nature. There was a king named Nebuchadnezzar who had taken Israel captive and was known for being a cruel ruler. One day he decided to build a massive golden statue of himself in his Kingdom. He then sent word to all the people and nations in his kingdom, regardless of social class or status, to come and hear the word he was going to declare. The declaration was simple: whenever you hear music of any kind being played, you are to fall down and worship the golden statue of the king. If someone was found in the kingdom not worshiping when the music was being played, they would immediately be thrown into a fiery furnace to be burned alive. The king wanted to test out his new ruling. So the music began to play and all the people in his kingdom fell down to worship the statue except three young men. Another tribe who was captive to Babylon told the king that three Jewish young men who were leaders in his kingdom were not bowing when the music was played. These three young men were named Shadrach, Meshach, and Abed-nego. We will pick up the rest of the story here in the Bible.

Then Nebuchadnezzar in rage and anger gave orders to bring Shadrach, Meshach, and Abed-nego; then these men were brought before the king. Nebuchadnezzar responded and said to them, "Is it true, Shadrach, Meshach, and Abed-nego, that you do not serve my gods or worship the golden image that I have set up? Now if you are ready. At the moment you hear the sound of the horn, flute, lyre, trigon, psaltery, and bagpipes and all kinds of music, to fall down and worship the image that I have made, very well. But if you do not worship. You will immediately be cast into the midst of a furnace of blazing fire; and what god is there who can deliver you out of my hands?" Shadrach, Meshach, and Abed-nego replied to the king, "O Nebuchadnezzar, we do not need to give you an answer concerning this matter. If it be so, our God whom we serve is able to deliver us from the furnace of blazing fire; and He will deliver us out of your hand, O king. But even if He does not, let it be known to you, O king, that we are not going to serve your gods or worship the golden image that you have set up." Then Nebuchadnezzar was filled with wrath, and his facial expression was altered toward Shadrach, Meshach, and Abed-nego. He answered by giving orders to heat the furnace seven

times more than it was usually heated. He commanded certain valiant warriors who were in his army to tie
up Shadrach, Meshach, and Abed-nego in order to
cast them into the furnace of blazing fire. Then these
men were tied up in their trousers, their coats, their
caps and their other clothes, and were cast into the
midst of the furnace of blazing fire. For this reason,
because the king's command was urgent and the
furnace had been made extremely hot, the flame of
the fire slew those men who carried up Shadrach,
Meshach, and Abed-nego. But these three men,
Shadrach, Meshach, and Abed-nego, fell into the
midst of the furnace of blazing fire still tied up. Then
Nebuchadnezzar the king was astounded and stood
up in haste; he said to his high officials, "Was it
not three men we cast bound into the midst of the
fire?" They replied to the king, "Certainly, O king."
He said, "Look! I see four men loosed and walking
about in the midst of the fire without harm, and the
appearance of the fourth is like a son of the gods!"
Then Nebuchadnezzar came near to the door of
the furnace of blazing fire; he responded and said,
"Shadrach, Meshach, and Abed-nego, come out,
you servants of the Most High God, and come here!"
Then Shadrach, Meshach, and Abed-nego came

out of the midst of the fire. The satraps, the prefects, the governors and the king's high officials gathered around and saw in regard to these men that the fire had no effect on the bodies of these men nor was the hair of their head singed, nor were their trousers damaged, nor had the smell of fire even come upon them (Daniel 3:13-27).

These young men reveal a confidence in the Lord that most believers have no grid for. They reveal what true hope is. We see in the story that regardless of the out-come they would not bow. They were faced with certain death, and their hope in God wasn't even connected to the outcome of their being saved. They confidently pro-claimed, "Whether God saves us or he doesn't, we will not bow." This is a picture of what it looks like for our hope to be in God and in His salvation, not in the expectation of an outcome. As we noted, the Jewish people had been taken captive, and some of the bright young men were brought into Babylon, and were being ruled over during this time. These three young men might never have even seen God do a miracle with their own eyes. If anything, they had only seen or experienced their nation being taken captive to Babylon. Talk about a letdown moment–a moment for your faith and hope in God to be shaken, and yet these three had hope and faith that God would not disappoint. This could only have come from them hearing from their parents and grandparents the mighty works of God that He had done for Israel in their history. For them to know that God had the power to deliver them, I propose, is connected to their ability to remember the testimonies of how God had delivered their nation before.

They found the God of all hope through the testimonies of what God had done in a different season–a season they were not even a part of. "For the testimony of Jesus is the spirit of prophecy" (Revelation 19:10b). As we remember what God has done in our history, in our family's history, and in the Church's history, we can strengthen our faith and hope that He can do something for the current situation we are facing. Our job is to wait on the Lord.

> Do you not know? Have you not heard? The Everlasting God, the Lord, the Creator of the ends of the earth does not become weary or tired. His understanding is inscrutable. He gives strength to the weary, and to him who lacks might He increases power. Though youths grow weary and tired, and vigorous young men stumble badly, yet those who wait for the Lord will gain new strength; they will mount up with wings like eagles, they will run and

not get tired, they will walk and not become weary. (Isaiah 40:28-31)

This idea of waiting on the Lord is not a passive waiting, wishing God would do something, the word "waiting" means to lie in wait; to look eagerly for.[3] It is an active posture of looking for the Lord in the midst of whatever situation you are facing. It is not a passive word meaning we should lie down in our sorrows. This verb "wait" is likened to a predator lying in wait to ambush their prey. We are called to actively wait and be aware of God and His Presence knowing that He will show up, our job is looking for where and when.

As we are discovering, hope in God in every season of life can be cultivated from a lifestyle of actively waiting and anticipating God to move in light of the testimonies of His power and greatness we have heard. Testimonies prophesy that Jesus wants to do again what has already been done. If He has healed a marriage before, healed a body, restored a family, blessed finances, restored something that was lost, redeemed a lost son or daughter, and the list goes on, He wants to do it again. But also keep in mind as you remember testimonies that Jesus never performed a miracle the same way. God loves to do similar things to reveal His nature, but He also is creative and does things in different ways. It is time we lean into the nature of God and anticipate how He is going to show up in our lives. It is time we allow the testimonies of His power and greatness to shape our faith and reveal the nature of Him in whom we place our hope. It is time to get our hopes up in a God whose very nature is good and kind. It is time to hope again!

Meditation Questions

1. Has my hope been in God's nature that is unchanging? Or has it been in an outcome I am expecting?

2. What testimonies have I personally experienced that revealed God's nature? What nature was revealed?

The Path Forward

1. Take a moment to ask the Holy Spirit if there is an area of disappointment in your life because of your hope being deferred. Journal any expectations of something specific that you have had that God never promised. Then take a moment to write down the nature of God that you are placing your hope in. Lastly, think of a testimony of God coming through in an area similar to the area you are believing for. Remember the testimony of Jesus, prophecies about who He is like.

Chapter 9:
Our True Identity

The pitter-patter of little feet running down the hallway to the kitchen-a familiar sound in the house that is usually followed by the pantry being opened where little hands are heard searching through drawers looking for the different surprises or tasty snacks. Once apprehended the doors are left open and the sound of a plastic wrapper being opened can be heard throughout the house along with the crunch of crackers being devoured as hunger is fulfilled. My wife and I have three children and this is a daily occurrence in our house. What I am always fascinated with is my children's confidence in what is available in the house.

They have an understanding of what is there and the confidence to access it when they want it. They are also aware of what they are not allowed to access in our house, or what they need permission for. My children understand they belong in our house and our family, and they are confident in their relationship with my wife and I. How do we become that confident in our relationship with God? Many believers are unaware of where they belong and what has been purchased and freely given to them. They battle lies thrown at them from the enemy to get them to fight for things that have already been given by the Father and tiptoe into places they already have access too.

Throughout this book, we have gone on the journey of discovering who God really is and how He has made a way for us to overcome pain in our lives so that we can walk in confidence and find true belonging; being fully seen, known, and loved by God. This is the place of intimacy with God in His glory. The next part on this journey is discovering how to sustain this new way of living by discovering the truth of who we were created to be, what we were created for, and recognizing the lies that don't align with the truth. I believe this is an essential piece in order to walk in belonging. We have to know the word of Truth about ourselves and God for us to truly love Him, us, and the world around us. Bill Johnson, Senior Leader of Bethel Church in Redding, CA says, "The greatest battle we will face is not between light and darkness, but between truth and lies."

What is the truth of how we were created and what is our true identity? What space were we created to belong in? And what do we have access to that has been freely given? To discover the answer to these questions we must look at the place where humanity was created and what was declared over us, our assignment, and what took place in the Garden of Eden. In the beginning, God created everything we see and experience, even things in the vast universe that no eye has ever beheld, and He called it all good. Then the sixth day came and something was different. He began by creating all the living things that would dwell on the land, from the great elephants to the insects that would crawl in the dust. He then said to the Spirit and Jesus His son,

> "Let us make man in Our image, according to Our likeness; and let them rule over the fish of the sea and over the birds of the sky and over the cattle and over all the earth, and over every creeping thing that creeps on the earth." God created man in His own

image in the image of God He created him; male and female He created them. God blessed them; and God said to them, "Be fruitful and multiply, and fill the earth, and subdue it; and rule over [every living thing on the earth]." ... And God saw all that He made on the sixth day and it was very good. (Genesis 1:26-28, 31)

Then the Lord God took the man and put him into the garden of Eden to cultivate it and keep it. The Lord God commanded the man, saying, "From any tree of the garden you may eat freely; but from the tree of the knowledge of good and evil you shall not eat, for in the day that you eat from it you will surely die." (Genesis 2:15-17)

God created a place for man to discover who He was and how man could walk with God in unbroken fellowship. He gave mankind an assignment and a boundary of what they could and could not access. Man was discovering his place in the presence of God. God continued with the creation of Eve and the last day of His creation ends with the epitome of belonging in the glory of God–the picture of human perfection in the presence of God. "And the man and his wife were both naked and were not ashamed"

(Gen. 2:25). Connection, acceptance, vulnerability, openness, and complete delight were the Garden's essence. Performance was not found, comparison did not exist, pain and isolation were not a reality, and the man and woman were both unashamed in the presence of God. This was the desire in God's heart as He created humanity–to walk with us and to delight in us as we delight in Him. So what went wrong?

I have often wondered why God would create such a wonderful earth, humanity to represent His likeness, and the expanse of the universe, just to place the devil on the same planet. And not only the same planet but to place the devil in the Garden and not tell man. If I had to place something in my house that could hurt my children, my first instinct would be to talk to them about the intensity of the item and how they are not to go near it. I would try to place a healthy "fear" of the item so that they would know it is not to be touched. Then I would lock the item up so that it would also be impossible for my kids to find it. Most of the Earth would call me a good parent for this. But would God? If out of fear and control, I did this, I would communicate to my kids I don't trust them and don't believe they would choose to obey. God chooses a different path–the ability to choose is the ability to love. There had to be a choice for Adam and Eve to choose to obey and love God or to obey another. But was God trying to set up humanity to fail? Actually, the complete opposite was at play. God had such belief in humanity, He was setting up a larger plan.

Our Adversary

Let's get back to the question, why did God place the devil and humans in the same garden at the very beginning? To fully understand this we have to find out more about our adversary. Yes, I did say our adversary. Many people think God and the devil are at war, and are equally powerful–that the devil represents darkness and God represents light. This couldn't be farther from the truth. The devil is a created being. He is not equal to God who is called the Beginning and the End, who created all things. The Bible commands us to "be of sober spirit, be on the alert. Your adversary, the devil, prowls around like a roaring lion, seeking someone to devour" (1 Peter 5:8). If he is our adversary then we have to get to know a little bit more about him, to understand our place in God's divine plan.

The devil was not his first name, nor his first calling. There was an angel named Lucifer who was one of only three archangels, or highest-ranking angels, recorded in the Bible. The Bible tells of his creation and fall, and the role he played. In Ezekiel 28 this prophetic word about Lucifer's fall is recorded:

You had the seal of perfection, Full of wisdom and perfect in beauty. You were in Eden, the garden of God; every precious stone was your covering: the ruby, the topaz and the diamond; the beryl, the onyx and the jasper; the lapis lazuli, the turquoise and the emerald; and the gold, the workmanship of your settings and sockets was in you. On the day that you were created they were prepared. You were on the holy mountain of God; you walked in the midst of the stones of fire. You were blameless in your ways from the day you were created until unrighteousness was found in you. By the abundance of your trade you were internally filled with violence, and you sinned; therefore I have cast you as profane from the mountain of God. And I have destroyed you, O covering cherub, from the midst of the stones of fire. Your heart was lifted up because of your beauty; you corrupted your wisdom by reason of your splendor. I cast you to the ground; I put you before kings, that they may see you. By the multitude of your iniquities, in the unrighteousness of your trade you profaned your sanctuaries. Therefore I have brought fire from the midst of you; it has consumed you, and I have turned you to ashes on the earth in the eyes of all who see you. All who know you among the peoples are appalled at you; you have become terrified and you will cease to be forever. (Ezekiel 28:12-19)

Lucifer was created to display perfection and beauty in the Presence of God. He was in the midst of the fire that is in the altar of heaven, the very throne of God. Yet, on account of his beauty, unrighteousness was found in him as his heart was lifted up because of his beauty. Another scripture gives us clarity on what took place found in Isaiah 14:11-16:

How you have fallen from heaven, O star of the morning, son of the dawn! You have been cut down to the earth, you who have weakened the nations! But you said in your heart, "I will ascend to heaven; I will raise my throne above the stars of God, and I will sit on the mount of assembly in the recesses of the north. I will ascend above the heights of the clouds; I will make myself like the Most High." Nevertheless you will be thrust down to Sheol, to the recesses of the pit. Those who see you will gaze at you, they will ponder over you, saying, "Is this the man who made the earth tremble, who shook kingdoms, who made the world like a wilderness and overthrew its cities, who did not allow his prisoners to go home?

Lucifer rejected how he was created and desired to obtain something he was never created for. He knew he was beautiful, and was aware of his perfection, yet he desired to be like God. **The pride of Lucifer that got him cast out of heaven, the pride that made him fall from the heights, the pride that changed his life forever, was the pride found in despising who he was created to be.** He despised being an archangel, he wanted to be something different. As we get this picture of our adversary, we realize he might be different than what we first expected. He rejected the Creator and the Creator's design for his life. This sin of pride is the very trap he places on the Earth. But where do we come into all of this? Let's go back to the Garden of Eden and creation. Why was it significant that we were made in the image of God? Because we were created with the very thing Lucifer desired but was never designed to walk in. Why does the devil hate humanity? We are created in the very way he desired to be, but could never access. We were made in God's image and in His likeness. We were designed to rule and reign over the Earth, and over the devil himself. We were to become a constant reminder of the life he was never going to have because of the pride in his heart and rejection of who he was created to be.

Unfortunately for humanity, the devil is cunning and thought he found a loophole in the design of God through the power-play of authority, obedience and getting mankind to question God's design for them. He used the very thing that got him thrown out of heaven to be the thing that would remove humanity from the Garden of Eden. Picking up in Genesis 3,

> Now the serpent was more crafty than any beast of the field which the Lord God had made. And he said to the woman, "Indeed, has God said, 'You shall not eat from any tree of the garden'?" The woman said to the serpent, "From the fruit of the trees of the garden we may eat; but from the fruit of the tree which is in the middle of the garden, God has said, "You shall not eat from it or touch it, or you will die." The serpent said to the woman, "You surely will not die! For God knows that on the day you eat from it your eyes

will be opened, and you will be like God, knowing good and evil." When the woman saw that the tree was good for food, and that it was a delight to the eyes, and that the tree was desirable to make one wise, she took from its fruit and ate; and she gave also to her husband with her, and he ate. Then the eyes of both of them were opened, and they knew that they were naked; and they sewed fig leaves together and made themselves loin coverings. They heard the sound of the Lord God walking in the garden in the cool of the day, and the man and his wife hid themselves from the presence of the Lord God among the trees of the garden. (Genesis 3:1-8)

The serpent was placed in the garden for man to rule over him. God gave man authority and dominion over every creeping crawling thing on the Earth, and the devil was one of those things. The problem was, God also placed the devil, humanity, and a command not to eat from a certain tree in the same place. Why? He did it to create a place of love and freewill. Without the ability for Adam and Eve to choose to obey God and understand how they were created, we would never have the ability to truly love God by choice. God desires people to understand who they are already created to be. Every person regardless of their knowledge of God is already created in His image. **The starting place of belonging is the understanding that we are designed in the image and likeness of God and created to walk with Him unafraid, unashamed, completely open, and free in His presence.**

This is a similar place that the devil had access to until he despised who he was created to be. In the same way he gets humans to despise themselves and how they are created. Since this moment humans have struggled with comparison, gossiping, tearing one another down, despising their own personality, gender, bodies, hair, face, and the list goes on and on. We continue to fall prey to the original sin of pride—the sin that somehow the magnificent Creator messed up with His creation, and somehow we need to change who we are to be able to find acceptance and belonging. As we see in the earth today there are movements of people that are rejecting who they were born to be or how they were designed thinking they are accessing full freedom and liberty. In reality they are being deceived by the same deception that led to the fall of our adversary. People have not realized that rejection leads to rejection, and pain leads to more pain. Belonging is found in acceptance of the truth of who we were created to be and the design God used in creation.

This understanding gives us confidence to approach the throne of grace with boldness (Hebrews 4:16), because it is the very place we are designed to be in. The devil tries to make people feel like they are missing something, not enough, or need to clean themselves up to find God and be accepted. Nothing could be farther from the truth. God created humanity with everything they need for life and godliness.

Honor is our Standard

This understanding of our creation and humanity's adversary hopefully will enable us to forgive quicker, love better, and walk more confidently in who we are. When we realize that everyone is made in God's likeness it is possible for us to honor everyone, even the person that the world would say doesn't deserve it. When we can forgive and honor people we have the ability to see who God made them to be rather than just their mistakes. Honoring a person because of how they are created paves a way for the fear of the Lord to live in our lives. Our understanding of His design for humanity sets us up to honor and value even if we disagree or dislike. The goal is to learn to value and love what God loves. Humanity is the apple of God's eye and the church is the bride for His Son. Honor is our ability to continue to remember these realities and treat people accordingly. Honor also sets us up to create unity and atmospheres of the glory of God on the earth. Honor is so powerful, because it takes faith and understanding in God to release it on the earth. It is not about agreement, performance, or connection, it is about leaning into God's value system and protecting it. **When we value what He values we attract His Presence in a room.** We see this in the life of Jesus. He constantly was found with people that society or the religious community wasn't honoring and broke the rules by walking with them, eating with them, and believing in them. From a tax collector becoming an apostle, to an adulterous woman being restored, to a pharisee being converted, Jesus honored humanity and God's value for people in the way they were created. This is what it looks like to walk in belonging with God and man.

Our Identity Restored

When Adam and Eve obeyed the devil, they handed the authority they were given over the Earth to him. The keys of the Earth were his, and from that moment on sin and chaos entered humanity. This was only solved through Jesus coming, paying the price of our sin, and living a blameless life so that His sacrifice would be sufficient in heaven to pay for our sin. Kris Vallotton, the Senior Associate Leader of Bethel Church in Redding, CA says it like this, "The Son of God had to become a son of man so that the sons of man could become Sons of God." The only way to defeat the devil and restore humanity was to become like a man and to do the opposite of what the devil had done.

> Christ Jesus, who, although He existed in the form of God, did not regard equality with God a thing to be grasped, but emptied Himself, taking the form of a bond-servant, and being made in the likeness of men. Being found in appearance as a man, He humbled Himself by becoming obedient to the point of death, even death on a cross. For this reason also, God highly exalted Him, and bestowed on Him the name which is above every name, so that at the name of Jesus every knee will bow, of those who are in heaven and on earth and under the earth, and that every tongue will confess that Jesus Christ is Lord, to the glory of God the Father. (Philippians 2:5-11)

This display of humility and His perfect sacrifice made a way for humanity to enter back into the presence of God.

But we do see Him who was made for a little while lower than the angels, namely, Jesus, because of the suffering of death crowned with glory and honor, so that by the grace of God He might taste death for everyone. For it was fitting for Him, for whom are all things, and through whom are all things, in bringing many sons to glory, to perfect the author of their salvation through sufferings. For both He who sanctifies and those who are sanctified are all from one Father; for which reason He is not ashamed to call them [brothers]. (Hebrews 2:9-11)

The sacrifice and exaltation restored the authority that Adam and Eve had given to the devil back to Jesus. Jesus then declares after the resurrection, "All authority has been given to Me in heaven and on earth" (Matthew 28:18).

Jesus fully restored what was lost in the garden. He restored our ability to fully belong in the Presence of God and to know what we have access to as His sons and daughters. He created the way for the veil that separated us from the glorious presence of God to be torn and for humanity to again have access to God's presence. He is the Way, the Truth, and the Life no one comes to the

Father except through Him (John 14:6). He restores our true identity and gives us access to become sons and daughters of God, confident in who He has created us to be, and confident that we belong in His presence.

Meditation Questions

1. What do I believe is my true purpose in life? Where am I destined to belong?
2. What are 5 things that I love about myself?
3. What are five things that I wish were different about myself? How does God see those things that I want to change about myself?
4. Is there someone in my life that I don't get along with? How can I start honoring them in a different way in the knowledge that they are made in the image of God?

The Path Forward

1. 30 Day Challenge: For the next 30 days ask the Holy Spirit what is one thing that He loves about you. Write each one down and review it after the 30 days to discover more of God's thoughts of love for you.
2. 10 Day Challenge: Think of one person who has a personality that annoys you and that you find hard to honor and love. For ten days ask God to speak one thing that He loves about how He made that person. Each day take 1 minute to pray and declare the thing you hear over that person. You might find a new heart towards that person as you do this.

Chapter 10:
Creating Places
of Belonging

It was 4:00am, and the stillness and quiet in the air would be deafening to some, but to me, it was calming. I was getting ready to start a shift stocking shelves at an office supplies store. It was just me and another employee that morning, and like most mornings, we kept to ourselves and didn't say much. Our job was pretty straightforward, unload the semi-truck full of pallets and stock the store before it opened by 10:00am. We had a great rhythm that more often than not resulted in us accomplishing this task with some time to spare. But there was one morning that was different and it took me years to understand why.

It was our usual 4:00am start, but at 5:00am the assistant manager of the store showed up. At first, it was business as usual, but then I started to notice myself feeling stressed out over that day's work. It became harder to focus on the simple task of stocking as I was starting to feel behind. I knew we weren't behind, but this feeling crept in. Throughout that morning, she would come and check in on how we were doing, and comment on if she thought we were actually going to get it all done before the store opened. Mind you, I did this many mornings, and my coworker and I never had issues before this. That morning we didn't get all the boxes of merchandise stocked before the store opened. That was also the first morning I felt stressed by the job, which had always felt like a calm, relaxing, and simple task.

What happened? Was it because the assistant manager was there and I wanted to get everything right? Or was something else happening that I was unaware of? Have you ever found yourself having an amazing day, and then in a moment, after you have stepped into another room or started to talk to a different person, or went into a different place in your city, your whole mood shifts and you even feel like your day is taking a different direction? This is the power of the spirit realm affecting the natural realm. This is another reality that can make us feel like we don't belong or can't access things we know are available to us. Most people I talk to almost always have a person on the other side of their problems. What if that person wasn't the problem? What if the thoughts in your head weren't always yours? If our battle isn't against humanity, but against the spiritual forces that impact humanity, then people aren't necessarily always the problem. It becomes easier to love people, and ourselves as we discover the right thoughts to listen to.

There are three realms that the Bible talks about that are active and alive that we live in whether we are aware of them or not.

First Heaven

The first heaven is the natural realm that we live in every day. It is the physical world that we engage with, go to work in, meet our friends in, and live life in. It is the world that was created in Genesis 1 when God walked through each day. He was crafting the natural realm and the place we as humans would take residency in. But this is just one of three realms that we engage with. It is the easiest realm to understand because it is the most visible of the three heavens. Every person on the earth believes in it and understands it, because it takes no level of discernment or insight to engage with it. But what are the other two realms and how do they play into our understanding of belonging, intimacy with God, and feeling confident in who He has created us to be?

Second Heaven

The second heaven is the spirit realm where angels and demons live. Paul references this realm in Ephesians when he says,

> Finally, be strong in the Lord and in the strength of His might. Put on the full armor of God, so that you will be able to stand firm against the schemes of the devil. For our struggle is not against flesh and blood, but against the rulers, against the powers, against the world forces of this darkness, against the spiritual forces of wickedness in the heavenly places. Therefore, take up the full armor of God, so that you will be able to resist in the evil day, and having done everything, to stand firm. (Ephesians 6:10-13)

Paul points out that our struggle will not be against humanity but something else that impacts humanity. This realm is at war over humanity. What are the different meanings of each of these spiritual forces that we are in struggle against?

"Rulers" in this verse is the Greek word "arche" which means "beginning or origin".[1] The first thing we are at war against is a dark spiritual force that tries to change the origin or original design and concept. We see this showing up across the nations where things that have a real meaning are being changed and humanity is buying it. "That's a fetus not a baby," "gender is fluid not biological," "I don't agree with that truth, so I will create my own," and the list goes on and on with areas in our culture that are being impacted by this dark spirit.

"Powers" is the Greek word "exousia" and means "the power of choice or the liberty of doing as one pleases".[2] It is the spirits of lawlessness that destroy the Earth. The influence on humanity to believe that their actions do not affect others or at least they don't care if they do. It is the epitome of selfishness and self-centeredness, and it is found in a spiritual power that tries to influence humans to behave in a way that destroys connection and belonging in relationships.

"World Forces of Darkness" is two words in the Greek. The first is "kosmokratōr" which means "the devil and his demons".[3] The second is "skotos" which means "darkness or blindness" and gives the metaphor of ignorance to the divine realm of heaven or hell.[4] Again we see Paul exhorting us with this reality. The devil is our adversary, not Jesus' or God's, and he aims to convince the world that the divine realm of heaven or hell does not exist. When we meet people who do not believe in a God we understand that they are being influenced by a world force of darkness that is hindering their ability to discover God. We have been commissioned to place the devil and these forces of darkness under our feet.

"Spiritual Forces of Wickedness" is two words, "pneumatikos" which means "the human spirit in relation to God"[5] and "ponēria" meaning "depravity, iniquity, wickedness, or malice".[6] These forces take the spirit of a man that is designed to serve God and influence him to walk in depravity of soul and iniquity against the Creator. It is the spirit that causes humanity to self-violate how they were created to be. It is the force that causes the nature of God in us to be distorted and destructive on the Earth.

Third Heaven

The third heaven is the realm where God's throne is. This is the place of complete holiness, beauty, and perfection, the place where John describes glory, awe, and wonder, filled with fear, trembling, and majesty.

> After these things I looked, and behold, a door standing open in heaven, and the first voice which I had heard, like the sound of a trumpet speaking with me, said, "Come up here, and I will show you what must take place after these things." Immediately I was in the Spirit; and behold a throne was standing in heaven, and One sitting on the throne. And He who was sitting was like a jasper stone and a sardius in appearance; and there was a rainbow around the throne, like an emerald in appearance. Around the throne were twenty-four thrones; and upon the thrones I saw twenty-four elders sitting, clothed in white garments, and golden crowns on their heads. Out from the throne comes flashes of lightning and sounds and peals of thunder. And there were seven lamps of fire burning before the throne, which are the seven Spirits of God; and before the throne was something like a sea of glass, like crystal; and in the center and around the throne, four living creatures...

and day and night they do not cease to say, "Holy, Holy, Holy is the Lord God, The Almighty, who was and who is and who is to come." (Revelation 4:1-6, 8)

This is the place the glory of God and His majesty are on display and where Jesus is positioned. "And He [Jesus] is the radiance of His [God's] glory and the exact representation of His nature, and upholds all things by the word of His power. When He had made purification of sins, He sat down at the right hand of the majesty on high" (Hebrews 1:3). Knowing this is the place of divine beauty, glory, perfection, and awe, where worship is constantly taking place, we have to ask ourselves, *where do we fit into this? Is this place for God alone? Is this place of His glory and majesty for me when I die?* The Bible speaks of one more mystery that changes our understanding of belonging, glory, and God. "But God, being rich in mercy, because of His great love with which He loved us, even when we were dead in our transgressions, made us alive together with Christ (by grace you have been saved), and raised us up with Him, and seated us with Him in the heavenly places in Christ Jesus" (Ephesians 2:4-5).

In Christ we have been given access to the throne of

grace, to encounter the Living God full of beauty, wonder,
majesty, and glory. We have been given access to expe-
rience the glory of God and live in His glorious presence.
This was what took place when Jesus breathed his last
breath and said "It is Finished" (John 19:30), "And yielded up His spirit. And behold, the veil of the temple was
torn in two from top to bottom" (Matthew 27:50-51). Jesus'
death gave us access again to the Holy of Holies, the very
throne of God. He gave us the ability to encounter God
in His glory and live in His glory; to "draw near with confidence to the throne of grace" (Hebrews 4:16). He opened
up the third heaven realm again for us to encounter God in
the splendor of His beauty, glory, and holiness.

Baseline as a Believer

The Spirit realm is living and active and is influencing people, places, and decisions constantly on the Earth. How
do we battle things we can't control and access things
we can't always see? It begins with discovering the baseline as a believer. What are my normal thoughts, feelings,
fears, insecurities, strengths, and connections with God
and others if I were having a normal day? To find this we
must be spending intimate time with God. Time that is full
of good things like worship, reading our Bibles, and pray-

ing. We need time that allows for a deeper connection to form. We must have intimacy with God.

Have you ever had a friend that you were close with that you could hang out without talking and still feel connected, or share a look in a public place to communicate what you were thinking? This is the desired intimacy God wants with each one of us–the place with Him where we can be silent and at rest in His presence and feel deeply connected. As we take time in His presence we discover our normal baseline of confidence, peace, joy, dreams, and hope for a future. We discover the true thoughts we have, whether good or bad, and His thoughts for us. This practice of silence in the Presence of God is different from a quiet time in the traditional sense. This space creates the ability for us to find belonging in His glory or what is holding us back from accessing it. Many times in silence my mind races with worries, things I have to get done, or people I need to forgive. That could either be a coincidence or I have finally given my heart space to reveal what is going on inside of me. The more I do this, the more aware I become of God's goodness and grace in my life, and the issues I am facing and overcoming. This creates my baseline and my ability to know what battles and thoughts I am currently fighting and which ones I am not. Why is this helpful?

Back to my story at the start of this chapter. That morning at the office supplies store, I was influenced by my assistant manager's struggles. Her anxiety and performance filled the atmosphere of that store and because I was unaware of this realm, it affected me and my day. I came under an atmosphere and a struggle that was never mine. The more we discover the presence of God and are open, vulnerable, and humble in His presence, the greater our ability to discover our baseline. As we discover this we become more equipped as a believer to "not conform to the world, but be transformed by the renewing of your mind" (Romans 12:2). We become powerful people who are aware of different atmospheres, and as we become aware we also learn how to not be influenced by them.

The last piece of belonging is to discover how to create belonging wherever we go. This requires a deeper understanding of what is coming against us and what we must face to create this reality of being fully seen, known, and loved by God and others. Will you find this with every human? No, and that is not the goal of this book. The heart is that you will find this first in your walk with God, and second in every place you are called to, and in every season of life you are walking through. There are four steps I will leave you with to start the journey of creating these places of breakthrough, freedom, confidence, and peace, these places of belonging wherever you go.

1. Become the Person Who Cultivates True Intimacy with God.

The first step is finding that silent place where it is just us and God where our hearts become aligned to His heart, and our hearts reveal what is actually going on inside of them. Then it is the act of telling God what He already knows about us. God knows everything but He delights in us trusting Him enough to open up to Him and reveal the pain, fears, doubts, and struggles we are walking through. Many people are scared to bring God into these areas out of a fear of judgment, but what does the Bible have to say about this?

> And there is no creature hidden from His sight, but all things are open and laid bare to the eyes of Him with whom we have to do. Therefore, since we have a great high priest who has passed through the heavens, Jesus the Son of God, let us hold fast our confession. For we do not have a high priest who cannot sympathize with our weaknesses, but One who has been tempted in all things as we are, yet

without sin. Therefore let us draw near with confidence to the throne of grace, so that we may receive mercy and find grace to help in time of need. (Hebrews 4:13-16)

Jesus is our great high priest who became one of us to understand our humanity and sympathize with our weaknesses. He came to be close to us, therefore, in our time of need we can boldly approach the throne. Too many believers in their time of need feel scared of the presence of God because they do not understand His nature, they still think He is going to reject them. God has done everything in His power to be close to us. It is time for us to believe it and step into it.

Beloved, let us love one another, for love is from God; and everyone who loves is born of God and knows God. The one who does not love does not know God, for God is love. By this the love of God was manifested in us, that God has sent His only begotten Son into the world so that we might live through Him. In this is love, not that we loved God, but that He loved us and sent His Son to be the propitiation for our sins. (1 John 4:7-10)

We have come to know and have believed the love which God has for us. God is love, and the one who abides in love abides in God, and God abides in him. By this, love is perfected with us, so that we may have confidence in the day of judgment; because as He is so also are we in this world. There is no fear in love; but perfect love casts out fear, because fear involves punishment, and the one who fears is not perfected in love. We love, because He first loved us. (1 John 4:16-19)

Understanding the perfect love of God and the intimacy He desires with us sets us up to not listen to the voice of judgment that tries to separate us and get us to hide from God. He desires for us to find perfect belonging in Him and intimacy with Him where nothing is hidden and everything is laid at His feet uncovered. This is the place where we are fully seen, known, and loved, for who He created us to be. This is the place where we find our confidence, purpose, and the reason we are alive. All of this is found in Him.

2. Become the Person That is Okay with Others Who are Walking Through Pain.

As we begin to cultivate this life of belonging ourselves, we are being set up to help others walk down the same road that we have walked. We become testimonies of hope. To do this well, we have to be okay with other people in pain. It is important to face our own pain first so we remove the fear of pain and gain compassion. Then, in a greater way, we can love the people in our lives that either go through seasons of painful situations, or begin to have pain from their past surface to be healed. We can no longer run from pain in others or separate ourselves from the pain of others. It is time we engage in the pain of others. It is time we become the good Samaritan.

> And a lawyer stood up and put Him [Jesus] to the test, saying, "Teacher, what shall I do to inherit eternal life?" And He said to him, "What is written in the Law? How does it read to you?" And he answered, "You shall love the Lord your God with all your heart, and with all your soul, and with all your strength, and with all your mind; and your neighbor as yourself." And He said to him, "You have answered correctly; do this and you will live." But wishing to justify him-

self, he said to Jesus, "And who is my neighbor?" Jesus replied and said, "A man was going down from Jerusalem to Jericho, and fell among robbers, and they stripped him and beat him, and went away leaving him half dead. And by chance a priest was going down on that road, and when he saw him, he passed by on the other side. Likewise a Levite also, when he came to the place and saw him, passed by on the other side. But a Samaritan, who was on a journey, came upon him; and when he saw him, he felt compassion, and came to him and bandaged up his wounds, pouring oil and wine on them; and he put him on his own beast, and brought him to an inn and took care of him. On the next day he took out two denarii and gave them to the innkeeper and said, 'take care of him; and whatever more you spend, when I return I will repay you.' Which of these three do you think proved to be a neighbor to the man who fell into the robbers' hands?" And he said, "The one who showed mercy towards him." Then Jesus said to him, "Go and do the same." (Luke 10:25-37)

We have to become the people that love well–the people that are on the road of life and stop when we come across someone in pain to help them get back up. This parable was in response to receiving eternal life and how we express the two great commandments. Jesus' answer reveals He is very interested in us helping one another in our times of need. And not just people we know and love, but people we have never met that can never repay us.

Let me clarify something. We need to step in and help people who cannot help themselves, but we also cannot work on someone's problems or pain in a greater way than they are willing to do themselves. We are not the savior or the healer. We are just a sign post and a servant of God's goodness and hope letting others know there is a God who heals completely, restores, and gives grace to all those who ask for it. Our job is to walk with people into healing, not walk for people.

3. Become the person who forgives as a lifestyle and helps others do the same.

Cultivating an unoffendable heart begins with a lifestyle of forgiveness. Forgiveness breaks down the walls of separation between individuals that keep us from belonging and unity. It is the very heart of God and compassion of God on display to the world. We cultivate this in people as we discover how to live without gossip and offense.

Gossip is one of the quickest ways to add fuel to unforgiveness. The spreading of information that is not ours to share cultivates mistrust, separation, drama, and ultimately secret offense that creates division. There is a sobering verse that reveals God's heart for us to live in a way that cultivates forgiveness and peace instead of disconnection and strife. "There are six things which the Lord hates, yes, seven which are an abomination to Him: haughty eyes, a lying tongue, and hands that shed innocent blood, a heart that devises wicked plans, feet that run rapidly to evil, a false witness who utters lies, and one who spreads strife among brothers" (Proverbs 6:16-19).

The Lord despised the spreading of strife and discord among brothers. It cultivates disconnection, offense, and disunity, ultimately hindering His glory from manifesting in that place. As we begin to cultivate belonging and a place of His glory on the Earth we must watch our tongues. If, in the beginning, God spoke and it was created and we are made in His image and likeness, when we speak what is being created? This is an important and sobering reality we all must live with.

> But no one can tame the tongue; it is a restless evil and full of deadly poison. With it we bless our Lord

and Father, and with it we curse men, who have
been made in the likeness of God; from the same
mouth come both blessing and cursing. My brethren,
these things ought not to be this way. (James 3:8-10)

Honor is key to cultivating these places of forgiveness and
truth. It is our responsibility to reveal the reality of God's
forgiveness in our lives to help one another choose to
forgive regardless of the painful scenario. Forgiveness is
essential in a person's process of healing and freedom,
yet too many people validate someone's unforgiveness
in the name of waiting until the person who hurt them
changes. Remember we are called to forgive and to teach
others to do the same regardless of the offender changing their ways. A lifestyle of forgiveness leads us toward
God's heart, where offense and disconnection do not live.
Forgiveness is the missing piece many believers are unaware of that is blocking them from true intimacy with God
and people.

**4. Become the Person Who Cultivates a Safe Place for
Others to be Seen, Known, and Loved.**
The final step to creating spaces of belonging is to cul-
tivate a safe place with the Holy Spirit for people to feel

seen, known, and loved. Discover the power of listening, not just talking. People think that information is what someone is looking for when many times they just need to be heard by someone. Our job is to become those people that listen. We listen to the person, but also we listen to what God is saying over the person and the situation. We lean into the wisdom of heaven.

Less talking and more listening will set us up to become safe places for people to open up. It does not mean we don't speak truth, but we must speak truth with love and compassion. The only way to find compassion is to stay close to God's heart and listen while hearing someone speak. The process of seeing someone to the point of them feeling known takes time and intentionality. Too often in our busy culture, we are on our phones, our minds are racing, we struggle to stay present in our own lives, and we have no capacity to be there for someone else. This is the moment to become the person that breaks that cycle in our day.

The road to belonging is not an easy one, but on the other side, I have not found a single person who didn't think it was worth it. Intimacy with God and one another is why we are alive. This is the moment to step into your purpose in life–to live whole, free, and alive. This is the moment to find your way back into God's glorious Presence in the perfect place of belonging with Him. Jesus gave everything to create a place for us to belong in Him. Now is the time to release this reality in the Earth. It is time for a movement of believers to find healing, intimacy, and belonging in the Holy Spirit–who walk in confidence that cannot be shaken and in authority to release belonging wherever they go.

Meditation Questions

1. Have you discovered your baseline in the Presence of God? If so, what is your normal?

2. What thoughts do you have in the presence of God and how do those thoughts change as you go throughout your day?

3. Is there someone in your life right now in pain that you have been avoiding instead of embracing?

The Path Forward

1. Take some time to dream about what it could look like to create a place of belonging within your life, friendships, ministry, workplace, or city? What steps can you take to reveal the glory of God through oneness with Him and connection to one another? Once you have your idea, take steps to execute what God has placed on your heart.

Endnotes

Chapter 2

1. "G3053 - logismos - Strong's Greek Lexicon (nasb95)." Blue Letter Bible. Web. 18 Aug, 2024. <https://www.blueletterbible.org/lexicon/g3053/nasb95/mgnt/0-1/>.

2. "G5313 - hypsōma - Strong's Greek Lexicon (nasb95)." Blue Letter Bible. Web. 18 Aug, 2024. <https://www.blueletterbible.org/lexicon/g5313/nasb95/mgnt/0-1/>.

Chapter 3

1. "H6588 - peša - Strong's Hebrew Lexicon (nasb95)." Blue Letter Bible. Web. 18 Aug, 2024. <https://www.blueletterbible.org/lexicon/h6588/nasb95/wlc/0-1/>.

2. "H5771 - āôn - Strong's Hebrew Lexicon (nasb95)." Blue Letter Bible. Web. 18 Aug, 2024. <https://www.blueletterbible.org/lexicon/h5771/nasb95/wlc/0-1/>.

3. "H4148 - mûsār - Strong's Hebrew Lexicon (nasb95)." Blue Letter Bible. Web. 18 Aug, 2024. <https://www.blueletterbible.org/lexicon/h4148/nasb95/wlc/0-1/>.

4. "H2250 - ḥabûrâ - Strong's Hebrew Lexicon (nasb95)." Blue Letter Bible. Web. 18 Aug, 2024. <https://www.blueletterbible.org/lexicon/h2250/nasb95/wlc/0-1/>.

5. "H7495 - rāpā' - Strong's Hebrew Lexicon (nasb95)." Blue Letter Bible. Web. 18 Aug, 2024. <https://www.blueletterbible.org/lexicon/h7495/nasb95/wlc/0-1/>.

Chapter 5

1. Kim, Jichan J., et al. "Indirect Effects of Forgiveness on Psychological Health Through Anger and Hope: A Parallel Mediation Analysis." Journal of Religion & Health, vol. 61, no. 5, Oct. 2022, pp. 3729–46. EBSCOhost, https://doi.org/10.1007/s10943-022-01518-4.

2. Kim, Jichan J., et al. "Indirect Effects of Forgiveness on Psychological Health Through Anger and Hope: A Parallel Mediation Analysis." Journal of Religion & Health, vol. 61, no. 5, Oct. 2022, pp. 3729–46. EBSCOhost, https://doi.org/10.1007/s10943-022-01518-4.

3. "Revile Definition.", Dictionary.com, 22 August 2024, www.dictionary.com/browse/revile

Chapter 6

1. Kim, Jichan J., et al. "Indirect Effects of Forgiveness on Psychological Health Through Anger and Hope: A Parallel Mediation Analysis." Journal of Religion & Health, vol. 61, no. 5, Oct. 2022, pp. 3729–46. EBSCOhost, https://doi.org/10.1007/s10943-022-01518-4.

2. "Matthew 18:24", Logos.com, ESV translation, https://app.logos.com/books/LLS%3AFSB/references/bible.61.18.22?linkSetId=A&tile=right&z-zls=2eMKcTcKNPQvDgjAURcO%2Fw4vCg24laSLCqGTCq05CwrfCjsOiw-pDCtsKvGMKaL8KTwrQgJcO%2Fw504w6l2w6%2FDoXLDrg4bwobCqM-KcBcOBasOww5LCom7CvcK%2FOmPCpMKdIsKIw7sOckxqQxApwqxY-w4Nrw4XDsAbCscKDD8OKBcKVSsOmTcOOdQEyPcKtNGUJdHBuwonCt-MOrw7rDqsOQMsOSwpATa2jDgBkDw5oRIx3DlMKgwrHDohfCjBs5M-sOCw47ChHPDuHMnwqXCvxrCjXMqWCvCu8O0wphuU0Ftw6nCv2fDhn-N%2Bw6QPW3hAQw%3D%3D

3. "Matthew 18:28", Logos.com, ESV translation, https://app.logos.com/books/LLS%3A1.0.710/references/bible%2Besv.61.18.23?linkSetId=A&tile=left&z-zls=2eMKcTcKMw4EKw4IwEETDv2XDgVttScKLIsK5VUEQesOrUTzCp-MOtakPDkyRuw5LCgsKEw7zCuxEvwr3DjTzDnkzCgBXDiUnCo8KBwrM-MwqzDkMKoamsvZsKewoUeHMOwe0jDkMKPWsOMCBzCisOOwpjDiR-VNw5PDrsKqw7rDmsKeC8OCJxLDqh5dw5HDiU5hfmQ5O8OIJcObw79D-dcKADMOeC8OSB3gAL8OVw6%2FChcOka8O0wokrwqnCpxbDvW1Iwqx-

Ow53CkjQkfVlZwosxCyB6L8OXwrTDsMK0w6DDpmbDo8KVMT7DohfCi-1hAFQ%3D%3D

4. "G3900 - paraptōma - Strong's Greek Lexicon (nasb95)." Blue Letter Bible. Web. 18 Aug, 2024. <https://www.blueletterbible.org/lexicon/g3900/nasb95/mgnt/0-1/>.

Chapter 7

1. "G3340 - metanoeō - Strong's Greek Lexicon (nasb95)." Blue Letter Bible. Web. 22 Aug, 2024. <https://www.blueletterbible.org/lexicon/g3340/nasb95/mgnt/0-1/>.

2. "Neuroplasticity", Psychologytoday.com, 22 August 2024, https://www.psychologytoday.com/us/basics/neuroplasticity

3. "Giving Thanks Can Make You Happier", Health.Harvard.edu, 14 August 2021, http://www.health.harvard.edu/healthbeat/giving-thanks-can-make-you-happier

Chapter 8

1. Kim, Jichan J., et al. "Indirect Effects of Forgiveness on Psychological Health Through Anger and Hope: A Parallel Mediation Analysis." Journal of Religion & Health, vol. 61, no. 5, Oct. 2022, pp. 3729–46. EBSCOhost, https://doi.org/10.1007/s10943-022-01518-4.

2. "H4900 - māšak̲ - Strong's Hebrew Lexicon (nasb95)." Blue Letter Bible. Web. 22 Aug, 2024. <https://www.blueletterbible.org/lexicon/h4900/nasb95/wlc/0-1/>.

3. "H6960 - qāvâ - Strong's Hebrew Lexicon (nasb95)." Blue Letter Bible. Web. 22 Aug, 2024. <https://www.blueletterbible.org/lexicon/h6960/nasb95/wlc/0-1/>.

Chapter 10

1. "G746 - archē - Strong's Greek Lexicon (nasb95)." Blue Letter Bible. Web. 22 Aug, 2024. <https://www.blueletterbible.org/lexicon/g746/nasb95/mgnt/0-1/>.

2. "G1849 - exousia - Strong's Greek Lexicon (nasb95)." Blue Letter Bible.
    Web. 22 Aug, 2024. <https://www.blueletterbible.org/lexicon/g1849/
    nasb95/mgnt/0-1/>.

3. "G2888 - kosmokratōr - Strong's Greek Lexicon (nasb95)." Blue Letter
    Bible. Web. 22 Aug, 2024. <https://www.blueletterbible.org/lexicon/g2888/
    nasb95/mgnt/0-1/>.

4. "G4655 - skotos - Strong's Greek Lexicon (nasb95)." Blue Letter Bible.
    Web. 22 Aug, 2024. <https://www.blueletterbible.org/lexicon/g4655/
    nasb95/mgnt/0-1/>.

5. "G4152 - pneumatikos - Strong's Greek Lexicon (nasb95)." Blue Letter
    Bible. Web. 22 Aug, 2024. <https://www.blueletterbible.org/lexicon/g4152/
    nasb95/mgnt/0-1/>.

6. "G4189 - ponēria - Strong's Greek Lexicon (nasb95)." Blue Letter Bible.
    Web. 22 Aug, 2024. <https://www.blueletterbible.org/lexicon/g4189/
    nasb95/mgnt/0-1/>.

About
Rory Helart

Thank you for reading my book *Belonging: The inner journey of being fully seen, known, and loved.*

A little about me…

I live in Redding, California with my beautiful wife Mari, and my three daughters.

I am the Youth Director for Young Saints at Bethel Church. My goal is to raise up this next generation in the wildness of the Holy Spirit, encountering His glory, and surrounded by the authentic power of the gospel of Jesus.

I have worked in youth ministry for over 15 years and am currently working on a Bachelor's Degree in Organizational Leadership.

Find more resources, podcasts, and opportunities to follow me at **roryandmari.com and my Instagram @roryhelart**

Made in the USA
Monee, IL
28 February 2025